WISCONSIN WOMEN IN THE WAR BETWEEN THE STATES

Facsimile of the 1911 Edition

WISCONSIN WOMEN IN THE WAR BETWEEN THE STATES

*Facsimile of the 1911 Edition
by Ethel Alice Hurn*

Foreword by Lance Herdegen

WISCONSIN HISTORICAL SOCIETY PRESS

Published by the Wisconsin Historical Society Press
Publishers since 1855

Foreword © 2013 by the State Historical Society of Wisconsin.
Originally published in 1911 by the State Historical
Society of Wisconsin.

For permission to reuse material from *Wisconsin Women in the War between the States: Facsimile of the 1911 Edition,* ISBN 978-0-87020-611-5, please access www.copyright.com or contact the Copyright Clearance Center, Inc. (CCC), 222 Rosewood Drive, Danvers, MA 01923, 978-750-8400. CCC is a not-for-profit organization that provides licenses and registration for a variety of users.

wisconsin**history**.org

This book is a facsimile reprint of the edition published in 1911. The pages of the original book were scanned electronically for reproduction; therefore any typographical errors or other irregularities in the original appear in this version as well.

Photographs identified with WHi or WHS are from the Society's collections; address requests to reproduce these photos to the Visual Materials Archivist at the Wisconsin Historical Society, 816 State Street, Madison, WI 53706.

Printed in Wisconsin, USA
Cover design by Ryan Scheife, Mayfly Design

17 16 15 14 13   1 2 3 4 5

♾ The paper used in this publication meets the minimum requirements of the American National Standard for Information Sciences — Permanence of Paper for Printed Library Materials, ANSI Z39.48–1992.

Front cover photo: Vignette carte-de-visite portrait of Jane (or Janet) Jennings, a Civil War nurse. She was raised in rural Green County, Wisconsin, and when her brother was wounded in 1863 she attempted to volunteer as a nurse but was turned down because at the age of twenty-four she was thought to be too young. After appealing to the head of army hospitals in Washington, DC, she was allowed to serve. At the age of fifty-nine she served again during the Spanish-American War. She died on December 31, 1917. WHi Image ID 32539

Cover background: © iStockphoto.com/thepalmer

FOREWORD

As the fiftieth anniversary of the American Civil War neared, the Wisconsin History Commission was established to develop and publish a series of "original papers" on Wisconsin's role in what was officially called the War of Rebellion. Picked as the sixth selection and published in May 1911 was *Wisconsin Women in the War between the States* by Ethel Alice Hurn. Five thousand copies were printed.

In many ways it was a landmark effort. Certainly it was one of the first formal recognitions—not only in Wisconsin but nationally—of the then overlooked and almost forgotten role Northern women played in 1861–1865. Reuben Gold Thwaites, superintendent of the State Historical Society of Wisconsin, noted in his brief introduction that thousands of writers had touched on "almost every phase of the struggle" to preserve the Union but "curiously enough, the part taken by the patriotic women of the North has thus far failed of adequate description."

The author of the study was Ethel Hurn of Oshkosh, then a student at the University of Wisconsin. Gathering the material for the book proved a daunting task. During the Civil War era women could not vote, hold bank accounts, or take a direct role in business. Nevertheless, in the time of national crisis, women took over farms and shops and other endeavors, and some left quiet family hearths to move onto the public stage. They prepared food, sewed and laundered, knitted socks and gloves, and organized campaigns and fairs as relief efforts that raised millions of dollars to aid wounded soldiers and assist war widows and orphans. However, these women's work was generally undertaken without thought of keeping a formal record. It could be found only in scattered collections of letters, newspaper files, several interviews, and the brief reports and pamphlets of soldier fairs and soldiers' aid societies.

But the author proved up to the task. Unfortunately, only little is known of Miss Hurn, who produced this important and significant work. A search by John Zimm of the Wisconsin Historical Society found that she apparently wrote no other books, "never married, had no children, and seems to have moved on to a lengthy career as a teacher after her work on the book was finished." She secured a teaching appointment in Oshkosh two years after publishing her work, then twelve years later began teaching at Edgewood High School in Chicago, where she spent twenty-nine years. According to a brief obituary in the *Chicago Daily Tribune* September 19, 1958, Ethel Hurn was seventy-seven when she died. She was survived by two brothers and one sister.

While the work of several well-known individuals, such as Cordelia A. P. Harvey, widow of Governor Lewis Harvey, and Mrs. Henrietta Colt of the Wisconsin Soldiers' Aid Society, was documented, Hurn concentrated her study chiefly on the thousands of average Wisconsin women who stepped forward. Thwaites correctly put the book into perspective: "With a tireless and courageous energy worthy of Spartan mothers, they kept the wheels of industry in motion, and thus saved the country from economic ruin. It is probable that future historians of the War may consider this the most important contribution of Northern women to the cause of the Union."

Of course, *Wisconsin Women in the War between the States* is just as significant today as it was a century ago because it documented an important turning point in the changing role of women in American society. Other scholars have added to the record in the passing years, but Hurn's groundbreaking book is welcomed back in print during this 150th anniversary of the American Civil War to be discovered and enjoyed as well as to enlighten a new generation of readers.

LANCE J. HERDEGEN
Chair, Wisconsin Civil War Sesquicentennial Commission
Walworth County, Wisconsin

WISCONSIN WOMEN IN THE WAR

CORDELIA A. PERRINE HARVEY
From a photograph in possession of the Wisconsin Historical Society

WISCONSIN HISTORY COMMISSION: ORIGINAL PAPERS, NO. 6

WISCONSIN WOMEN IN THE WAR BETWEEN THE STATES

BY ETHEL ALICE HURN, B. A.

WISCONSIN HISTORY COMMISSION
MAY, 1911

FIVE THOUSAND COPIES PRINTED

Copyright, 1911
THE WISCONSIN HISTORY COMMISSION
(in behalf of the State of Wisconsin)

Opinions or errors of fact on the part of the respective authors of the Commission's publications (whether Reprints or Original Narratives) have not been modified or corrected by the Commission. For all statements, of whatever character, the Author alone is responsible

DEMOCRAT PRINTING CO., STATE PRINTER

Contents

	PAGE
WISCONSIN HISTORY COMMISSION . .	xiii
EDITOR'S INTRODUCTION	xv
AUTHOR'S NOTE	xix

WISCONSIN WOMEN IN THE WAR:

Chapter I. The departure of the Regiments	1
A rally	2
Drilling recruits	6
Flag raising	7
Flag presentations	9
Banquets for the soldiers . . .	11
Chapter II. Soldiers' Aid Societies . .	18
Sanitary Commission	18
Misdirected energies	21
Aid Societies formed	22
The Societies at work	25
Knitted articles	29
Packing the boxes	30
Wisconsin regiments supplied . . .	31
Contributions for local companies . .	33

CONTENTS

	PAGE
A Milwaukee donation	34
Aid Societies discouraged	36
The National spirit grows	39
Difficulties surmounted	41
Scurvy combatted	42
Amount contributed	46
Chapter III. The Wisconsin Soldiers' Aid Society and Mrs. Henrietta Colt	49
Visits to Southern hospitals	51
Milwaukee Society enlarged	54
Chamber of Commerce	55
Generous contributions	56
Work for soldiers' wives	57
Chapter IV. Conditions at Home	61
Gaieties checked	62
Provision for volunteers' families	63
Destitution at home	64
Promises forgotten	67
Philanthropic spirit	69
Pathetic incidents	71
High prices	73
The greater sacrifice	74
Women as farmers	78

CONTENTS

	PAGE
Women in new lines of work	83
The sewing machine	85
A patriotic school teacher	86
Confederate prisoners	87
Extravagance rebuked	89
Chapter V. Letters for the Front	92
Letters for strangers	95
Letters from the field	96
Difficulties of letter writing	97
Chapter VI. Women with the Regiments	99
Daughters of the regiment	100
In masculine garb	102
Officers' wives	104
Mrs. Lyon's services	106
Deaths of women in the army	107
Chapter VII. Hospitals and Nurses	108
Early hospitals	108
Women as nurses	110
Opposed by surgeons	110
Wisconsin nurses	112
Sanitary agents	117
Chapter VIII. Mrs. Cordelia A. P. Harvey	118
Early life	118

CONTENTS

	PAGE
Governor Harvey's death	119
Sanitary agent	122
At Cape Girardeau	123
Secures reforms	125
Influence with officials	127
At Memphis	129
Brings sick soldiers to the North	131
Inspects hospitals	131
Chapter IX. Mrs. Harvey's interview with Lincoln	134
Seeing the President	135
Interview with Stanton	136
The President unconvinced	137
Mrs. Harvey successful	140
Northern hospitals	143
Soldiers' Orphans' Home	144
Chapter X. The Christian Commission	148
Religious awakening	149
Women's auxiliaries	150
Wisconsin Commission	150
Experiences of Wisconsin women	151
Reading material	153
Criticisms	154

CONTENTS

	PAGE
Chapter XI. The Northwestern Sanitary Fair	155
Preparations	155
German women's participation	157
Wisconsin contributions	158
Chapter XII. The Milwaukee Soldiers' Home and the Soldiers' Home Fair	161
Milwaukee Soldiers' Home	162
First year's results	164
Soldiers' Home Fair	165
The Governor aids	167
Wisconsin towns assist	167
The Fair building	169
The exhibits	170
Schools contribute	170
Special features	172
Financial success	174
Merged in Government Home	174
INDEX	177

Illustrations

	PAGE
Portrait of Cordelia A. Perrine Harvey . *Frontispiece*	
View of Camp Randall at Madison, in 1861	12
In the Office of a Soldiers' Aid Society	24
Women in the Field, in war-time	78
In front of a Field Postmaster's Tent	94
Wisconsin Soldiers' Orphans' Home at Madison	144
United States National Soldiers' Home at Milwaukee	174

WISCONSIN HISTORY COMMISSION

(Organized under the provisions of Chapter 298, Laws of 1905, as amended by Chapter 378, Laws of 1907 and Chapter 445, Laws of 1909)

FRANCIS E. McGOVERN
Governor of Wisconsin

CHARLES E. ESTABROOK
Representing Department of Wisconsin, Grand Army of the Republic

REUBEN G. THWAITES
Superintendent of the State Historical Society of Wisconsin

CARL RUSSELL FISH
Professor of American History in the University of Wisconsin

MATTHEW S. DUDGEON
Secretary of the Wisconsin Library Commission

Chairman, COMMISSIONER ESTABROOK
Secretary and Editor, COMMISSIONER THWAITES
Committee on Publications, COMMISSIONERS THWAITES AND FISH

INTRODUCTION

Fifty years have passed since the Confederate attack on Fort Sumter. The story of the terrible War between the States, which followed that dramatic episode, has been told by thousands of writers, who have touched on almost every phase of the struggle. But curiously enough, the part taken by the patriotic women of the North has thus far failed of adequate description. Their hearts responded to the appeal of the Union as quickly and as nobly as those of the men. At first, however, their opportunities for service did not equal their eagerness to help; but it was soon realized that woman's office in the conflict was of its kind as important as that of the marching rank and file. They lent encouragement and helpful sympathy in a hundred practical ways. They not only sanctioned but urged the enlistment of their fathers, sons, brothers, and lovers. They ministered to organized companies and regiments before the departure for the front. When once the volunteers were in the field, boxes of dainties and comforts were sent to them from home; and the ill and wounded appealed especially to the boundless charity of womankind.

At first the efforts of the women were unorganized and individual. But as the fruit of experience, their leaders devised and carefully managed an admirable system of organized aid and relief. The result was an incalculable assuagement of the miseries of war. To accomplish these sanitary and curative results, large funds were needed. Here again the organizing ability of women, never more conspicuously evidenced, came into play. Every possible source of revenue was drawn upon. Particularly profitable were the great fairs and exhibitions which they held in important centres of population.

Women likewise were found at the front as nurses, hospital matrons, sanitary agents, Christian Commission workers, and occasionally as "Daughters of the Regiment" or as officers' wives. But the heaviest burden undoubtedly was carried by those who remained at home. In addition to their much-needed work of relief, many labored steadily upon the farms and in the shops, as breadwinners for their families, while the men were serving in the ranks. The extent of their co-operation in this direction can never definitely be ascertained. With a tireless and courageous energy worthy of Spartan mothers, they kept the wheels of industry in motion, and thus saved the country from economic ruin. It is probable that future historians of the War may consider this the most important contribution of Northern women to the cause of the Union.

Early in its career, the Wisconsin History Commission arranged to present at least a summary statement of the share of Wisconsin women in these several lines of wartime activity. The task of collecting and classifying the data, and presenting it in literary form, was (under the general direction of the Committee on Publication) undertaken by Miss Ethel Alice Hurn of Oshkosh, at that time a student in the University of Wisconsin. The Commission now takes pleasure in publishing this interesting and valuable study, which amply justifies her selection for so difficult a task.

Difficult, because testimony concerning the four years' war-work of the women of our State was not easy either to discover or to interpret. Their deeds were performed merely as a matter of duty or heartfelt desire, with no thought of proclaiming them to the world. Miss Hurn's material could be found only in scattered contemporary correspondence and subsequent reminiscence, in pamphlet reports of fairs and societies, in newspaper files, and in verbal statements and letters obtained by her from survivors. From these disassociated bricks and mortar of history, she has constructed her edifice. The result is an unusual presentation of the sympathetic and sanitive forces underlying the terrible stress of war. She has given especial emphasis to the work of one or two women of unusual ability, whom circumstances placed in positions of national importance. But the record is chiefly that of the average woman, who with cheerfulness and fidelity approaching the heroic, met and grappled with the problems forced upon her by the War. The Commission believes that this record will not be received with indifference in the homes and at the hearthsides of the Wisconsin people of our own day.

The index is the work of another Wisconsin woman, Dr. Louise Phelps Kellogg, of the editorial staff of the Wisconsin Historical Society. Her family traditions connect her closely with the sanitary work of Milwaukee women during the giant contest that not only "tried men's souls" but fired the hearts of their womenkind.

R. G. T.

WISCONSIN HISTORICAL LIBRARY
May, 1911

AUTHOR'S NOTE

The author is under special obligations to Mrs. James Selkirk of Clinton for access to the Harvey manuscript. Among many others, the following have also been of much assistance in this undertaking: Mr. Peter Van Vechten and Mrs. Caroline Bell of Milwaukee, Miss Mary E. Simmons of Beloit, Mrs. Martha Showalter of Lancaster, Hon. H. W. Rood and the late Judge E. W. Keyes of Madison, Mrs. Mary B. Robison of Topeka (Kansas), Miss Mary A. Lapham of Oconomowoc, and Mr. A. C. Wallin of Prairie du Chien.

Throughout the work, frequent and helpful suggestions have been received from Drs. F. J. Turner, C. R. Fish, and R G. Thwaites of the Department of History in the State University. The last named, in the capacity of Editor of the Wisconsin History Commission, has with great care prepared the manuscript for the press and supervised its publication.

E. A. H.

Wisconsin Women in the War

Chapter I

The Departure of the Regiments

After the firing on Fort Sumter the North suddenly awoke to a realization that civil war was inevitable, and prepared accordingly. From a peaceful, industrial community Wisconsin was quickly transformed into a hive of military activity. Every town, village, and hamlet became a recruiting station, and whenever enlistments were mentioned, a thrill ran through every community.

Under such circumstances the proclamation of Governor Randall, April 22nd, 1861, to the "Patriotic Women of Wisconsin" was peculiarly inspiring. In it he said:

> I know that you will respond cheerfully to my request that you contribute your aid in the present crisis, in the way of preparing lint and bandages for the use of the army. A much larger amount of such necessaries for an army may be prepared, than may be required by the sons of Wisconsin, but in the long war likely to follow, there may be thousands who will require such kindness. * * *
>
> It is your country and your government as well as theirs that is now in danger, and you can give strength and courage and warm sympathies and cheering words to those who go to do

WISCONSIN WOMEN IN THE WAR

battle for all that is dear to us here. Bitter as the parting may be to many, I am assured that you will bid them go bravely forward for God and Liberty, to "return with their shields, or on them." I commend the soldiers to your kindness, encouragement and prayers, with full confidence that when occasion calls, many, very many Florence Nightingales will be found in our goodly land.[1]

No one can doubt the patriotism and enthusiasm of the women of those days. They entered heart and soul into every conceivable activity of the time. They followed Governor Randall's advice—scraped lint, made bandages, and encouraged men to enlist. Many war-meetings were held in southern Wisconsin, which were attended by women as well as by men.

A Rally

A typical rally was usually conducted as follows. A few days beforehand a notice was sent to the people of the district, announcing that a war-meeting would be held at a certain time and place, that a well-known orator would speak, and that there would be "an abundance of martial music on the programme." On the evening chosen, such members of the local company as desired to go, entered wagons provided for the purpose, and formed a procession moving through the town with colors flying, drums beating, accompanied by much cheering. In the meantime a crowd having assembled at the place of meeting, cheered lustily as the soldiers dismounted, to which the latter responded, and much enthusiasm was evoked. A recent writer thus describes such an occasion:

---

[1] Official publication in *Wisconsin State Journal* (Madison), April 23, 1861.

DEPARTURE OF THE REGIMENTS

After the teams had been cared for, and all were settled in the school-house, as a matter of course some music would be called for, and there, while the shrill tones from Rube Green's fife would almost pierce holes through the window panes, Trume Hurlbutt, seeing the admiring gaze of all the country maidens centered upon him, would fairly astonish them by his dexterity in handling the sticks; and Jim Solomon would so belabor his old bass drum that the loosened plaster would drop from the ceiling. [2]

The effect of the music upon the audience was instantaneous; all were thus put into the best possible frame of mind for hearing the "ringing address of the captain, the next thing on the programme." Then followed calls for more music, succeeded by more cheers. At this psychological moment the captain would give a hearty invitation for the young men to join the company, whereupon a deep silence generally fell upon the audience, for while it was easy enough to use their lungs in such a cause, actual enlistment was a very serious matter.

At this point in the meeting the young ladies were generally more enthusiastic than the boys, whether because of their more intense patriotism, or because, however wrought up they might become, concerning the duty of enlistment, they were safe from any personal appeals to put down their own names, I do not pretend to say. We all knew that, as a matter of course, every good girl was a patriotic girl, and equally well we knew, that had every girl of them desired to enlist, not one of them would be accepted. [3]

Now and then a young girl would add her powers of persuasion to those of the captain, and would urge the

---

[2] H. W. Rood, *Company E and the Twelfth Wisconsin in the War for the Union* (Milwaukee, 1893), pp. 47, 48.
[3] *Ibid*, pp. 49, 50.

WISCONSIN WOMEN IN THE WAR

boys to enlist, hinting that a young fellow who was as brave and plucky as John would surely not need coaxing; this was a most trying situation for the poor fellow, who probably wished at the moment that both he and his girl had stayed at home. At one such meeting a certain young girl became very enthusiastic and

> cheered with the men and boys, clapped her hands every time the captain made a particularly good point, and waved her handkerchief at the band when they played "The girl I left behind me." When stirring exhortations to enlist were brought to bear upon the young men, she became more expressive and enthusiastic than ever. At last she spoke right out in meeting as follows: "John, if you do not enlist, I'll never let you kiss me again as long as I live! Now you mind, sir, I mean what I say."[4]
>
> Poor John! he had no sort of notion of enlisting, but his patriotic girl had put before him an alternative that made him fairly tremble with indecision. But John's misery was the cause of much merriment in such a crowd at such a time; especially it amused the members of our company, and they exhorted him something after this fashion: "John, you'd better go with us! Come now, John, if I were in *your* place I'd enlist, before I'd give up, what you've got to."[5]

But it was quite evident that John had lost all interest in the meeting and that he stubbornly refused to enlist. History does not divulge whether or not the patriotic girl kept her vow.

Although this was the usual type of a rally, methods differed in different towns. In some places a choir both of men and women would begin the exercises with bright and lively songs to arouse enthusiasm, then change to more quiet and plaintive tunes to evoke the patriotism of those

---

[4] *Ibid*, p. 50.
[5] *Ibid*, pp. 50, 51.

DEPARTURE OF THE REGIMENTS

it was hoped would enlist. After this occurred, the singers would again burst jubilantly into patriotic melodies.

Such rallies were frequent during the earlier years of the war; and while not always successful in securing enlistments, they were valuable in arousing the community to seriously consider the war and its issues. The following is an instance well calculated to show the spirit of the women who attended such meetings:

There was an enthusiastic war-meeting a few miles from our town. Just before the speaker arose to address the audience, a good old lady rose to her feet and said she had five sons now in the army, fighting to maintain the nation's honor, and another son about sixteen, whom she would gladly send as a drummer boy, whose health would not permit him to fight. Also her husband had just enrolled his name. "And now," said she, "I propose three cheers for our good old flag!" and with those words she walked up and kissed the flag that she had yielded her heart's treasure to sustain. [6]

Another patriotic woman in speaking of her husband said, "I would almost despise my husband and would think him a sneak, if he hadn't gone." The following circumstance illustrates a fine type of patriotism and religious faith. A woman from Vernon County accompanied her husband to the place of enlistment, to see him sign his name to the enlistment roll, since he was determined to go. As he laid down the pen, she took it up and wrote "God bless and protect you, my husband."[7] But it remained

---

[6] *Correspondence of Wisconsin Volunteers* (newspaper clippings, chiefly soldiers' letters), collected by E. B. Quiner, in Wisconsin Historical Library.

[7] Dan Webster and Don C. Cameron, *Story of First Wisconsin Battery* (Washington, D. C., 1907), p. 7.

WISCONSIN WOMEN IN THE WAR

for a Waushara County woman to cap the climax by saying, in a burst of patriotic fervor, that if she had another husband, she would send him also. So it may be assumed that Wisconsin women were as patriotic and courageous in giving up their soldiers, as the latter were in marching away to fight for their country.

Drilling Recruits

Everywhere, in small villages as well as in towns and cities, the task of drilling recruits was busily going on, and everywhere people old and young were filled with enthusiasm and delight for all things military. Even in the village, there was "generally more or less a crowd at hand to witness [the evolutions of the soldiers] and hear the soul-stirring and ear-splitting music of the fife and drum."[8]

While recruiting was going on, daily drills were held on the town square, where keeping step to Union music was vigorously practiced. "Officers and men alike were ignorant of military tactics, and all studied with zealous determination to master the art of war. The park became an attractive place—attractive to the young ladies as well as to recruits; to the former [because] they could see the soldier boys, and to the latter [because] there the girl he was to leave behind him was sure to be."[9]

There, too, the presence of women was effective, for "when the soldiers were on the drill-ground under the admiring gaze of a score of bright eyes, they stood up straighter and taller and looked manlier than ever before,

---
[8] Rood, p. 42
[9] Webster and Cameron, p. 7.

DEPARTURE OF THE REGIMENTS

and as a matter of fact * * * always got in their best work when they had a bevy of admiring maidens for spectators."[10]

Not only in villages did women turn out to watch the soldiers, but the same interest was manifested in towns and cities. This is shown by the remark made by a soldier at Camp Utley, Racine: "We marched along Racine's most aristocratic streets, and every man did his best, for the walks were filled with the belles of that fair city."[11]

Flag Raising

When this wave of enthusiasm for things military and patriotic swept over Wisconsin, a strong desire was created to fly the American flag.

Such a display of the national colors had never been seen before. Flag raising was the order of the day. The trinity of red, white, and blue colors were to be seen in all directions. Shop-keepers decked their windows and counters with it. Men wore it in neckties or in a rosette, pinned on the breast or tied in the button-hole. Women wore it conspicuously also. The bands played only patriotic airs, and "Yankee Doodle," "Red, White, and Blue," and "Star Spangled Banner" would have been worn thread-bare, if possible.[12]

The flag floated not only from halls, stores, dwellings, school-rooms, churches, doors, windows, and dining-rooms, but even adorned the parlors of cultivated women.[13] It is not surprising, therefore, to find that flag-making was

---

[10] Rood, p. 42.
[11] Webster and Cameron, p. 16.
[12] J. H. Billings, *Hard Tack and Coffee* (Boston, 1888), p. 42.
[13] William DeLoss Love, *Wisconsin in the War of the Rebellion* (Chicago, 1866), p. 125.

WISCONSIN WOMEN IN THE WAR

the order of the day. In every town and city women were busy making flags for the different military companies. These were of various materials and designs, and each bore some inscription to distinguish it from others. One interesting flag is thus described:

> It is of dark blue silk with a silver fringe. On one side is painted a shield, inscribed "Racine 1861," with a national flag draped on either side of it, surmounted by an eagle, holding the bolts of Jove. Above is the motto "Remember Sumter!" On scrolls near the center is written, "For Freedom and for God." On the reverse is a shield with a star, surrounded by military emblems with the name of the company inscribed. [14]

A Lancaster banner, on a background, profusely adorned with rosettes, bore the inscription, "Lead is our King, not Cotton."[15]

Another flag from the same town was made of cream-colored linen with the following inscription in large black letters: "Lead mines of Grant. We are called. We have come. Wisconsin." The other side of this banner was made of blue silk, and bore the inscription, "We pledge our lives, our fortunes, and our sacred honor."[16] Not every banner was made of silk, however; for one, worthy of mention, was of merino, its staff being surmounted by a globe. This one had specific interest, because the young girls who made it gave up the joys of dancing for the soberer pastime of sewing.

The flags thus far described were not national, but designed as emblems for local companies. United States flags

---

[14] *Corres. Wis. Volunteers*, i, p. 73.
[15] *Ibid*, p. 72.
[16] Ms. letter of Mrs. Martha Showalter, Lancaster.

DEPARTURE OF THE REGIMENTS

were also occasionally presented, although these were usually furnished by the State.

After the fall of Fort Sumter the pupils of the Beloit High School were filled with enthusiasm and said, "We must have a flag." "So the boys bought the material, and the girls made it, our principal bidding us 'not to make the stitches so long that the birds would catch their feet in them.' "[17] The women of Beloit also desired to make a United States flag, but were told that the Government would furnish it; "and besides," added the women, "if we made it as big as our hearts, no color sergeant could carry it."

A unique flag, and one that savored of Revolutionary days, was made in a little country village and raised July 4, 1861. The women of the family made the stripes of muslin and turkey-red calico, and a piece of the daughter's blue apron (for cotton cloth was dear) formed the background for the stars, which were six-pointed and patterned after a drawing by the younger son. The flag-pole was made by a son, home on sick leave, and so the flag represented the united efforts of the whole patriotic family.[18]

Flag Presentations

Since so many flags were made by the women for the departing troops, it is not surprising that almost every town had its formal flag presentation, on which occasion the people gathered together to listen to "words of tenderest

---

[17] Ms. letter of Mary E. Simmons (Beloit, March 4, 1910).
[18] *Sheboygan Telegram* (December 2, 1909).

WISCONSIN WOMEN IN THE WAR

encouragement, spoken by some young girl with cheek and heart aglow." [19]

The presentation of a flag to the First Wisconsin Regiment by Mrs. George Walker, in behalf of the ladies of Milwaukee, occurred at Camp Scott on May 8, 1861. The speech was made in the presence of the Governor, Brigadier-General King, and other Wisconsin officers. After a review of the regiment a hollow square was formed, and Mrs. Walker was introduced to the troops. [20]

The following sentences of her address reflect the spirit of the occasion:

In confiding this banner to be upheld by your strong arms and dauntless hearts, we feel that you will never permit a hostile or traitor's flag to assume the place of the glorious and unsullied stars and stripes, which have been, with the blessing of God, and ever shall be, a symbol of our national glory. * * *

The ladies, who have prepared this beautiful standard, have adorned its azure field with a star for each state of the Union, making thirty-four in all. We have made no distinction, selecting some and excluding others, but have embraced our whole country with all its luminaries shining, for we can recognize no secession from the glorious sisterhood of states. [21]

Such speeches filled the listening soldiers with an intense patriotism, which the following quotation well expresses: "Not one but resolved to face even death with unflinching nerve, and to always keep in mind as their watchword, 'Death before dishonor.'" [22]

---

[19] Mrs. S. E. Henshaw, *Our Branch and Its Tributaries* (Chicago, 1868), p. 20.

[20] Love, p. 213.

[21] *Ibid*, p. 214.

[22] *Corres. Wis. Volunteers*, i, p. 24.

DEPARTURE OF THE REGIMENTS

Banquets for the Soldiers

In many towns the departing soldiers were served with special luncheons or suppers, which were much appreciated by the local companies. These were particularly noteworthy in Milwaukee, Madison, Racine, La Crosse, Oshkosh, and other places where camps were located. On Thanksgiving, Racine women furnished the men in camp with a Thanksgiving dinner, at which twelve hundred doughnuts, five hundred pies, and a hundred and seventy-five turkeys were eaten. A soldier who attended this banquet wrote: "We had cold turkey, roast chicken, apple, pumpkin, and mince pies, sponge cake, pound cake, and indeed everything the most fastidious could wish for, and above all, the ladies seemed to take a special delight in smiling upon us, while we were eating."[23]

Perhaps the most ambitious attempt of this sort was made at Madison in July, 1861. The patriotic men and women of the city and surrounding country met at Assembly Hall in the Capitol, and resolved to entertain the Fourth and Fifth regiments. The plan was, that the women from the country should furnish the substantial part of the menu, including chickens, lambs, boiled ham, vegetables, butter, cream, eggs, and cake; while the Madison women brought jelly, pies, and other delicacies. Six thousand people attended this banquet, many of them from Middleton, Cottage Grove, and Sun Prairie. They came in wagons and carriages with waving banners and music, bringing their provisions, which the Madison women received and disposed of. Meanwhile, the soldiers at Camp

---

[23] *Id.*, ii, p. 76.

WISCONSIN WOMEN IN THE WAR

Randall had decorated the grounds for the occasion, by making designs of white sand, bordered with pebbles. Among the figures were hearts, diamonds, circles, flags, and shields—each company having a different emblematic device. Among the inscriptions were: "Rebels, blow your horn;" "Ladies of Dane, the Beaver Dam Rifles appreciate your kindness;" and "Remember Sumter!" The most elaborate attempt at decoration was made by Company E. "Here was an elevation of an immense circle, in the center of which was the Wisconsin coat of arms, badger and all. This was a most elaborate piece of work, showing superior taste and skill. The badger, like all the devices about the grounds, was made of pebbles and presented a very fair animal. Around the circle were the words, 'Janesville Light Guard. Deeds not words.' The whole was tastefully decorated with nuts, green and dry." [24]

These indefatigable workers had also decorated the dining-hall with bushes and leaves. Thus the whole affair presented a most festive appearance. But the supper must not be forgotten. A writer described it as follows:

Precisely at five o'clock everything was in readiness, and the signal for supper was promptly responded to by the entrance of the twenty companies into the dining hall. Before commencing the feast, each company in turn gave three rousing cheers for the ladies, and then the order for three cheers by the two regiments together was given, and such cheers and tigers as were raised, are seldom heard. The best efforts of two thousand throats were given to the work, and as evidence that it was successful, these cheers were distinctly heard in all parts of the city, a distance of a mile and a half. There was good feeling there and a great amount of it. [25]

---

[24] *Id.*, i, pp. 210, 211.
[25] *Ibid*, p. 211.

VIEW OF CAMP RANDALL, AT MADISON, IN 1861
Printed from a contemporary wood-engraving in possession of the Wisconsin Historical Society

DEPARTURE OF THE REGIMENTS

After supper the women were thanked for their sumptuous entertainment and then the regiments were drawn up for dress parade, and a flag was presented to each. Subsequently, other entertainments were provided, and the grand finale was a dance upon the parade grounds, "in which the sturdy soldiers and the fair damsels participated in high glee. * * * It was truly a happy day. The weather was delightful, the ladies were agreeable, the soldiers were gallant, and the outsiders in general were pleased with everything. * * *,We can only add, that the whole affair was a perfect success; and to the ladies of the country and the city be awarded all the credit. God bless them all." [26]

Such elaborate entertainments as the foregoing were infrequent; yet on a smaller scale the same sort of thing was being done in almost every village or town, for departing soldiers, whose letters are full of appreciation for such kindnesses. Oyster suppers, strawberry festivals, and the like were the favorite modes of entertainment and often a programme followed, as for example, when the Sauk County riflemen left home. Thirty young girls, tastefully dressed in white, sang a national anthem, after which the volunteers proceded to Kingston, where a reception and feast were given them.[27] Dances were also a popular form of farewell to the soldiers. These were usually held in the town hall, where a crowd of friends and relatives gathered to make merry with them. But the effort at cheerfulness was not always successful, for occasionally a devoted couple would be seen dancing, while tears ran down their cheeks.

---
[26] *Ibid*, p. 211.
[27] *Ibid*, p. 231.

WISCONSIN WOMEN IN THE WAR

One onlooker at such a gathering expressed the sentiment of the assembled company when she said, "I feel as though I were going to dance on their graves."

Not content with doing everything possible for the companies from their own towns, Wisconsin women offered every possible courtesy to the stranger companies marching through. When the Seventh Regiment passed through Janesville on its way to Chicago, there were huzzas, a waving of handkerchiefs, and something more substantial. As the two trains drew up alongside of each other, pails of coffee and buckets of sandwiches, pies, cakes, and apples were quickly distributed. [28]

At Kenosha a most successful entertainment was given the First Regiment in June, 1861. A volunteer wrote:

After a short march to a small grove, we ate an excellent dinner, prepared by the ladies. This was by far the most pleasant time we have had since our enlistment. Everything that we could wish for in the shape of pies, cakes, and meats were furnished in abundance. The ladies filled the knapsacks of the different companies with biscuits, meat, and cheese. [29]

Occasionally bouquets were bestowed upon the departing regiments, and even more intimate tokens; for "sometimes girls passed along the side of the car, shaking hands with their 'brothers all,' and occasionally some bold soldier boy, with a spice of fun or tenderness in his heart, would bring the face near enough to imprint a chaste salute." But the tables were turned when a daring maid kissed the entire membership of a local company, from the

---

[28] *Ibid*, p. 272.
[29] *Ibid*, p. 20.

DEPARTURE OF THE REGIMENTS

captain with his whiskers to the humblest private in the ranks.

A large and handsome cake was given to Company A by the Milwaukee women, accompanied by a splendid bouquet which bore the inscription, "Flowers may fade, but the honors of the brave never." [30]

Sometimes the companies in the various State camps received gifts from their home towns, and occasionally relatives from home visited them. On May 24, 1861, the Kenosha boys at Camp Scott were cheered by the visit of nearly a hundred Kenosha women, who came laden with a bountiful supply of "cuisine dainties, prepared to tickle the palate and make glad the heart." [31]

Visitors at the various camps became more numerous as the time for the companies to depart drew nigh, and painful scenes were often witnessed by sympathetic onlookers. A correspondent wrote:

We almost daily witness thrilling scenes, not blustering, but calm heart-moving ones, of parents visiting their sons * * * brothers and sisters visiting brothers, or pretty wives often with their pretty babes, visiting their husbands, each bringing the soldier a few of the common luxuries of home as a remembrance. See him accompany her to the gate, where he must stop—goodbye, goodbye, they pass along, and he looks so steady, so sober, but his eyes begin to glisten, as he turns away with a heart too full, a throat too choked for utterance; perhaps it is the last goodbye to the dearest on earth.[32]

Such a parting is but a type of what occurred in every home or camp, where a soldier was leaving his beloved ones.

---

[30] *Ibid*, p. 239.
[31] *Ibid*, p. 8.
[32] *Id.*, vii, p. 4.

WISCONSIN WOMEN IN THE WAR

Usually the women were brave—O! so brave—only to break down later, when they were sure that an exhibition of grief would not unnerve the man whose courage they had tried so hard to sustain. In one case a soldier came back to get some forgotten article only to find the mother who before him had been so brave, sobbing uncontrollably, while the little brother lay weeping in her arms. But such scenes ought not to be reported. They should be imagined rather than expressed. It is enough to say, that these women, when they pinned on the rosette of red, white and blue, or gave the little Testament to their brave boys, were making fully as great sacrifices for their country as the departing soldiers.

An account of the demonstration in Milwaukee at the departure of a regiment is recorded as follows:

> The sympathy of Milwaukee citizens has been shown to us in the brightest light. I did not see a single window in all the streets we passed, without being filled both by males and females; the latter gracefully waving their handkerchiefs or bidding us farewell and success; among whom many a slender, blue-eyed beauty came to our view. A multitude of men, women and children followed us to the depot. [33]

When the Twenty-fourth Regiment left Milwaukee, a densely packed mass of men, women, and children waited patiently from eight o'clock in the morning until one, when a sudden shower scattered them all for a time. At three o'clock the crowd gathered again, and thousands came to say goodbye to acquaintances, friends, or relatives. "Cheer after cheer went up as they went down Main street [now Broadway], and the Newhall blossomed out with white

---

[33] *Id.*, viii, p. 55.

DEPARTURE OF THE REGIMENTS

handl̲̲̲̲̲̲̲̲̲̲̲̲̲̲̲̲̲̲̲̲̲ depot there were at least seven thou̲̲̲̲̲̲̲̲̲̲̲̲̲̲̲̲̲̲̲ e limited space about the cars was all̲̲̲̲̲̲̲̲̲̲̲̲̲̲̲̲̲̲̲̲̲siastic friends, shaking hands and sa̲̲̲̲̲̲̲̲̲̲̲̲̲̲̲̲̲̲̲̲̲ough such a scene seemed cheerful ̲̲̲̲̲̲̲̲̲̲̲̲̲̲̲̲̲̲̲̲̲̲xcited over the prospect of his ̲̲̲̲̲̲̲̲̲̲̲̲̲̲̲̲̲̲̲̲̲̲, there were plenty of shadows to ̲̲̲̲̲̲̲̲̲̲̲̲̲̲̲̲̲̲̲̲̲. A writer tells the following pathetic story:

As the men passed into the cars, a young girl, plainly dressed, approached one of the windows. Hiding her face in her hands, and too much awed by the crowd to sob aloud, she gave way to silent tears. A middle-aged man, a private near the farther limit of the age for military-service, appeared at the car window, toward which the girl was drawn, and took off his cap with a trembling and unnerved hand, while silent tears coursed down his weather-beaten cheeks. A father was apparently bidding his child an unspoken farewell. [34]

From the foregoing, it appears that the women of Wisconsin were as patriotic as the men during the days when the regiments marched away; their courage was even greater, for:

> Heroic males the country bears
> But daughters give up more than sons.
> Flags wave, drums beat, and unawares
> You flash your souls out with the guns
> And take your Heaven at once!

> But we!—we empty heart and home
> Of life's life, love! we bear to think
> You're gone,—to feel you may not come,—
> To hear the door-latch stir and click;
> Yet, no more you! . . . nor sink. [35]

---

[34] *Id.*, x, p. 331.

[35] Elizabeth Barrett Browning, "Parting Lovers," in *Complete Poetical Works* (Cambridge edition, 1900), p. 446.

Chapter II

Soldiers' Aid Societies

When Lincoln in April, 1861, issued his first call for troops, the women throughout the country held meetings to confer with regard to the best means of organized help for the soldiers. In many ways this was a remarkable movement. Tradition, custom, instinct, and the isolated life in small communities broken into separate religious sects, opposed a general union Nevertheless, regardless of creed or social position, women began at once to form a national organization to minister to the army. [36]

Sanitary Commission

The Women's Central Association of Relief, formed at New York in April, 1861, was the first step toward the organization of the United States Sanitary Commission. [37] President Lincoln failed at first to realize the great benefit to be derived from such an organization; he described it as a "fifth wheel to the coach," but finally he gave his consent to the formation of a "Commission of inquiry and advice with respect to the sanitary interests of the United

---

[36] Ida M. Tarbell, "The American Woman," in *American Magazine* (April, 1910), p. 811.

[37] Rossiter Johnson, *Short History of the War of Secession* (Boston, 1888), pp. 352, 353.

SOLDIERS' AID SOCIETIES

States forces." June 13, 1861, this committee received from Lincoln and Simon Cameron (at that time Secretary of War) an order authorizing the formation of the Sanitary Commission.

The object of the Sanitary Commission was to do what the Government could not accomplish. The latter undertook to provide all that was necessary for the soldier, whether sick or in good health, whether in active service or in the hospital. But from the very nature of things, this was an unrealized ideal. The Commission was to meet the emergency caused by the breakdown of governmental machinery; it made provision for all needs, and sought always to supplement, never to supplant the Government. It never forgot that it must be subordinate to army rules and regulations; that it must not under any circumstances break down the essential military discipline on which so much depended. [38]

The work of the Commission was comprehensive in its scope, including many lines of usefulness. It sent medical inspectors to the army to report on sanitary conditions and administration, prepared eighteen treatises on the best means of preserving health in camps, put trained nurses into the hospitals, established soup depots, and invented hospital-cars for a more humane transportation of the wounded. It had also a general relief-department, with twelve branch depots in the large cities; each of these had auxiliaries, engaged in obtaining supplies. The special relief department established forty lodges for sick soldiers; these were scattered along the route of the army. It

---

[38] Mary E. Livermore, *My Story of the War* (Hartford, Conn., 1889), p. 129.

WISCONSIN WOMEN IN THE WAR

founded claim, pension, and back-pay agencies, and printed a hospital directory. Most invaluable was its system of battlefield relief, through which thousands of dollars worth of sanitary supplies were distributed after the great battles.[39]

Although the administrative responsibility of this organization was assumed by men, it was the women of the North who were the bone and sinew of the Commission, for by their generous contributions and patriotic spirit they kept it alive. From an historical standpoint the organization, although outside the Government, assumed certain governmental powers and duties. From a humane standpoint it expressed the blended charity of all the loyal states, gathered and organized according to a carefully studied method approved by the Government, guaranteed efficiency, economized energy, and secured continuance of the generous love, looking out with aching eyes and waiting hands from almost every home throughout the land.[40]

The Chicago branch of the Sanitary Commission, because of its convenient location, became the channel through which most of the supplies from Wisconsin were sent to the front. On October 17, 1861, this branch was organized, and almost immediately the women of the Northwest began to send large donations to its quarters. The energy, earnestness, and patriotism of these women of the Northwest was admirable as was shown by letters received by the Sanitary Commission, which came from cities, towns, villages, and prairie settlements, and were in themselves a "monument

---

[39] *Ibid*, pp. 130–132.

[40] U. S. Sanitary Commission *Bulletin* (New York, 1886), i, pp. 289, 290.

SOLDIERS' AID SOCIETIES

to the patriotism, ability, and culture of the writers."[41] Requests for instructions show a remarkable clearness of thought. These emanated from every point, and were actual reports of admirably organized societies, whose business methods were so good that the exclamation, "The Northwest is full of wonderful women!" was quite justified.

Misdirected Energies

While companies were forming and departing, one resolute purpose lay deep in the heart of every Wisconsin woman; namely, to do all possible to bring comfort and encouragement to the departing regiments. Such a strong feeling did not remain long unexpressed. A period of misdirected effort was the result—misdirected in the sense that the women failed to realize that they were doing harm in persistently sending boxes of jellies and sweetmeats to men who were undergoing the process of acclimatization, and also misdirected when their time and labor were spent on unnecessary and useless articles, such as havelocks. Societies were even formed for this purpose alone, their expenses being defrayed by "havelock sociables." Not until bales of havelocks were made did they realize that the gifts were useless, and that the men received them with merriment and put them to every possible use, except the one for which they were intended, namely as a protection for the head from the hot rays of the sun.[42]

These early efforts likewise did not aim at the broader patriotism, which seeks to benefit the sick or wounded

---

[41] Henshaw, p. 22.
[42] *Ibid*, pp. 20, 21.

WISCONSIN WOMEN IN THE WAR

soldier regardless of his company, regiment, or state. As time passed, however, Wisconsin women realized their mistakes, and like the other loyal women of the North, were as anxious to rectify them as they had been headlong in perpetrating them.

Aid Societies Formed

Shortly after war was declared, Wisconsin women began to meet to make garments for the soldiers. These gatherings were at first spontaneous and could hardly be given a name. They were prompted by the exigencies of the time and animated by the thought that several enthusiastic, industrious women could accomplish more when working together than separately. As time went on, and the influence of the Sanitary Commission grew stronger, such gatherings became regular aid societies, with officers, rules, and a definite scheme of operation. This was accomplished all the more easily, because many Wisconsin women were used to similar church organizations, and like their New England sisters had long worked in missionary and sewing societies. As a rule the women who had been prominent in the earlier organizations, became the leaders in the aid societies, so that the movement in Wisconsin went rapidly forward.

Although the aid societies were informal during the first years of the war, a definite scheme for conducting them had been evolved by 1863; this did much to increase their efficiency.[43] According to this plan the women who wished to organize a society determined upon a certain day and

---

[43] "Women's Central Association of Relief," in U. S. Sanitary Commission *Bulletin*, ii, pp. 370, 371.

SOLDIERS' AID SOCIETIES

place for a public meeting; all the women and the young girls of the neighborhood were invited to attend. Ministers were asked to announce this invitation from the pulpits, and a notice was placed in the post office. The object of the societies was to provide for the comfort of sick and wounded soldiers of the United States Army. The officers were as follows: a president, five vice-presidents, a secretary and treasurer, a committee on cutting, and another on packing.

The duties of the president were to preside at all meetings, to have the general interests of the society in charge, and to purchase all materials. Her duty it was likewise to present a plan for the ensuing month, after having consulted with the vice-presidents and the treasurer. One of the vice-presidents was to preside in the absence of the president; all five, in connection with the president and the secretary, were to devise means for improving and increasing the usefulness and efficiency of the society. At the meetings one of the vice-presidents distributed the work, supervised it generally, and collected it again. It was also the duty of the vice-presidents to canvass the village and neighborhood for the purpose of securing as many members as possible.[44] It was suggested that a division into districts would facilitate the work. This proposal was accepted, and the vice-presidents in their respective districts explained the object of the society and endeavored to enlist the women's sympathy in its behalf. It was decided that no membership fee should be required.

The secretary-treasurer was to keep all the books of the society and conduct a correspondence with "that branch of the Sanitary Commission to which the supplies were to be

[44] *Ibid*, pp. 370, 371.

WISCONSIN WOMEN IN THE WAR

sent." Her duty it was to write to the Commission for any information which might be desired by members of the society.

The cutting committee was to cut material into garments, according to approved patterns, and to have a sufficient quantity of work prepared for every meeting. The packing committee was to elect its own chairman, who was to make a detailed and accurate list of the contents of each box, while it was being packed. This list, with the name of the society written on it, as well as the name and post office address of the secretary, was to be placed immediately under the cover of the box or the barrel, while a duplicate invoice was to be sent without delay, to the secretary, who was to notify the Sanitary Commission by letter, of the consignment. Every box or package was to be distinctly addressed and marked on the outside with the name of the town or the village from which it was sent.

Meetings were to be held weekly or fortnightly at the option of the society. It was considered best to hold them in some regular place of assembly, such as the town-hall, court-house, public school-house, or church-vestry.[45] In one of the Wisconsin towns the aid society was sorely tried, for the mayor was a copperhead, and he forced the women to pay rent for the use of a room in the city hall.

The plan of organization has been fully described because it illustrates the excellent business sense of its originators,[46] and explains how these aid societies were able to accomplish such results.

In Brodhead, Wisconsin, a most interesting experiment

---

[45] *Ibid*, pp. 370, 371.
[46] This outline plan was prepared by Louisa Lee Schuyler.

IN THE OFFICE OF A SOLDIERS' AID SOCIETY

From sketch by Thomas Nast, in F. B. Goodrich, *The Tribute Book* (N. Y. 1865), p. 111

SOLDIERS' AID SOCIETIES

was tried, the formation of a young people's society called the Alert Club. The object of this club was to furnish funds for the aid society, of which it was an auxiliary. According to its plan the village was to be divided into ten districts with four collectors for each. Twenty cents a month were to be collected from each woman, and as much as possible from each man. The collectors were to secure the subscriptions on the first Monday of each month, and to pay over the money to the aid society on the following Monday. Entertainments of various sorts, such as lawn sociables and strawberry feasts, were also to be given in order to raise money; and if the young women desired, they could make garments for the soldiers. This was not an obligatory duty, however, as the main purpose of the club was to provide funds for the mother society.

The Societies at Work

The work done at these meetings was of all sorts; but first and foremost lint was scraped, and for this purpose old table-cloths, rags, and even linen brought from former homes in the old country were used. One method of preparing the lint was to lay a plate bottom upward, on a table or on the lap of the operator, and to place a piece of linen on it; this was vigorously scraped with a case-knife until it was transformed into a fluffy mass of fibre.[47] Another method, which was to ravel the linen, was perhaps less strenuous. Thousands of bandages were likewise sewed and rolled up, ready for use. At the beginning of the war these were the two chief occupations; the women realized that

---
[47] J. H. Waterman, "Rosendale Squad," in *National Tribune*, May 3, 1900.

WISCONSIN WOMEN IN THE WAR

bales of lint and bandages would be needed after each battle. It is needless to say, that had absorbent cotton been in use at that time, much labor might have been saved for other duties. The lack of modern pharmaceutical supplies, during the war, would appal a person living in this generation. It is difficult for us to realize how far surgery and the science of medicine have progressed during the last fifty years, although we know that in the Civil War period antiseptics were not commonly used, and few of the numerous conveniences and appliances which are in use today, could be resorted to.

Among the articles made at the aid societies were quilts and blankets, many of which had some cheering message, or the name of the maker sewn in them. Occasionally an interesting correspondence was started by this means. One Wisconsin quilt had a curious history. It was made in 1864 by the women of Green Bay, and sent to the army, where for twenty years all track of it was lost. Finally, in 1884, it was discovered in the cabin of a negro family living near Bentonville. The piece that remained contained eight blocks, each of which had in the centre a white cross running diagonally, while the outside pieces were of colored calico, bordered with white. On each square was written the name of its maker in indelible ink; a few of the blocks bore also timeworn inscriptions. [48]

These verses illustrate the sturdy and uncompromising spirit of the makers of the quilt:

> For the gay and happy soldier
> We're contented as a dove,
> But the man who will not enlist
> Never can gain our love.

[48] *Milwaukee Telegraph*, Jan. 9, 1884.

SOLDIERS' AID SOCIETIES

If rebels attack you, *do* run with the quilt
And safe to some fortress convey it;
For o'er the gaunt body of some old secesh
We did not intend to display it.
* * * * * * *
'Twas made for brave boys, who went from the West;
And swiftly the fair fingers flew,
While each stitch, as it went to its place in the quilt,
Was a smothered "God bless you, boys," too. [49]

The comfort-bag or housewife, familiarly known as "hussy," was so much a necessary part of every well-provided soldier's equipment, that a detailed description may not be out of place. It was a small bag or needle-case containing half a dozen assorted needles, a skein of white cotton, a skein of black linen thread, half a dozen horn or porcelain shirt buttons, a dozen trouser buttons, a small ball of yarn, a darning needle, and a few pins. [50] Occasionally some careful mother or wife would add a small bottle of cayenne pepper, a package of court-plaster, or perhaps a bottle of quinine, which was thought at that time to be a panacea for all the ills that flesh is heir to. [51]

It would be impossible to overestimate the value of such a bag to a soldier in active service. One Wisconsin aid society received five hundred letters of thanks for the two thousand three hundred bags which it had sent out. Among these correspondents was one who declared that his housewife had been "worth ten dollars" to him.

Another soldier wrote to thank the women of Janesville

---
[49] *Ibid.*
[50] U. S. Sanitary Commission *Bulletin*, ii, p. 760.
[51] J. M. Aubery. *Thirty-sixth Wisconsin Infantry* (Milwaukee, 1900), p. 12.

WISCONSIN WOMEN IN THE WAR

for seventy or eighty beautiful needle-books "elegantly wrought and of invaluable utility." He further states, that soldiers have the poorest clothes of any class of people, yet are required to make them do the most service, and that the needle-books are in great requisition on Saturday nights, as the soldiers must then prepare for the Sunday morning inspection. [52]

Blankets, quilts, and comfort-bags were not the only articles made by the aid societies; all kinds of clothing, such as shirts, dressing gowns, underwear were prepared, the material for such articles being bought with the society's money. Flannel shirts seem to have been especially popular, for the women of Watertown made five hundred for the local company. In a few cases the aid societies even made uniforms for the soldiers, but this was only done occasionally during the first few months of the war. The Milwaukee Zouaves, for instance, were presented with fatigue uniforms consisting of brown trousers, hickory shirts, and red caps. [53]

In order to illustrate what was done in the various aid-societies, the following testimony is quoted:

> They made flannel blouses and shirts; if I remember aright, these were gray, as we knew that it was the safest color. But as the South had preempted that color, when more regular equipment was adopted our boys were given the next best, the light blue.
>
> Both real flannel and cotton-flannel undergarments were made, and one woman was so expert in cutting, that she seriously strained her thumb, plying the shears. Good woolen socks were knit, or fished out of the home stock in baskets. Chests were

---

[52] *Corres. Wis. Volunteers*, v, p. 79.
[53] *Id.*, i, p. 2.

SOLDIERS' AID SOCIETIES

ransacked for the substantial blankets that were woven on the looms of our mothers and grandmothers. Quilts were made and given. I remember giving away my pieced blocks, having a double thought, to do service and to get rid of finishing up the quilt. [54]

Knitted Articles

A very popular as well as a necessary occupation was the knitting of socks, mittens, and gloves, especially a peculiar kind of mitten, which had a forefinger as well as a thumb, so that it could be used in shooting. This knitting occupation was kept up in public as well as in private, for women knitted while traveling, during spare minutes at home, or at the meetings of the aid society. One patriotic woman threw her religious scruples to the wind, and knitted a few rounds on Sunday before the church-bell rung. Even young girls knitted socks, and their grandmothers toed and heeled them. In fact there was a perfect epidemic of knitting, which lasted throughout the war.

Among the articles received by Wisconsin soldiers in 1862 were numerous pairs of mittens. "And if they could see the caps flying and hear the cheers that are sent up for the ladies of 'Old Grant' upon the receipt of these articles, they would feel well repaid for their trouble." [55] Another soldier wrote:

A box of mittens from the ladies of Milwaukee was distributed by our returned chaplain on Thursday afternoon, and were just in time to do good service. The boys now gladly take the "mitt" from the girls they left behind them. May God prosper the good ladies of Milwaukee in their work of kind deeds. Their

---

[54] Ms. letter from Miss Simmons.
[55] *Corres. Wis. Volunteers*, iii, p. 277.

WISCONSIN WOMEN IN THE WAR

gifts touch the rough soldier's heart and call forth many prayerful thanks and thoughts of loved firesides they have left, to struggle for union and liberty.

Packing the Boxes

Besides making garments and knitting socks it was the pleasant duty of the aid societies to fill boxes with good things to eat, and many were the glasses of jelly, cakes, pastries of all sorts, meats, and every conceivable delicacy, which were packed together with clothing, books, and newspapers. J. H. Billings says in his *Hard Tack and Coffee:*

> The art of box-packing must have culminated during the War. It was simply wonderful, delightfully so, to see how each little corner and crevice was utilized, not stuffed with paper (by those who understood their business), thus wasting space, but filled with a potato, an apple, an onion, a pinch of dried apples, a handful of peanuts, or some other edible substance. These and other articles filled crannies between carefully-wrapped glass jars or bottles of toothsome preserves, or boxes of butter, or cans of condensed milk, or well-roasted chickens, and the turkey each box was wont to contain. If there was a new pair of boots among the contents, the feet were filled with little notions of convenience.
>
> There was likely to be, amid all the other merchandise already specified, a roll of bandages and lint. It added greatly to the pleasure of the investigator to come upon a nicely-wrapped package, labeled "from Mary," "from Cousin John," and perhaps a dozen other relatives, neighbors, schoolmasters, most of which contributions were delicious surprises, and many were accompanied by notes of personal regard and good wishes. [56]

It is interesting to read of the boxes received by Wisconsin companies in 1861, and to note the contents and the

---
[56] *Op. cit.*, p. 221.

SOLDIERS' AID SOCIETIES

comments made thereon. It seems that when the army was to remain in one place for two or three weeks, the average soldier mailed a letter home to his mother, father, wife, sister, or brother, and stated carefully what he would like to have sent in a box at the earliest possible moment, giving with great precision the address, to be written on the cover.[57]

Wisconsin Regiments Supplied

Shortly after the battle of Bull Run an appeal came to the women of Racine, stating that there was a great shortage of linen for the sick and wounded, and as a result of the battle the hospital would be overflowing with men.

So the women of Racine met at the Presbyterian Church one evening to arrange for the making of garments for the sick and wounded in the hospitals at Washington. The material purchased was to be taken to the old *Advocate* reading-room in the Masonic Building, where it was to be cut out and delivered to those who wished to lend a helping hand.[58]

In October, 1861, a cavalry company stationed at Ripon sent a most appreciative acknowledgement of the thirty-two quilts and blankets given them by the women of Berlin.[59]

A soldier of the Seventh Regiment writes in November, 1861, that the idea of raising money for blankets and clothing is a fine one, but that the Government supplies two heavy overcoats, one heavy roundabout, etc., and that these

---

[57] *Ibid*, p. 217.
[58] *Corres. Wis. Volunteers*, i, p. 118.
[59] *Id.*, ii, p. 66.

WISCONSIN WOMEN IN THE WAR

are quite enough to carry in one knapsack. He continues his comment by saying: "If privations should come later, we would be glad to avail ourselves of the opportunity of drawing on the liberality and kindness of the good folks of our native homes." [60]

A letter from a member of the First Regiment, on the other hand, contains an appeal to the ladies of Jeffersonville and Port Fulton to provide blankets and other comforts for the sick soldiers. [61] The First Regiment had been longer in the field and had presumably seen more active service than the Seventh, which may explain the different points of view.

A letter written in 1861 by a Beloit soldier to the people of his town, contains an almost pitiful appeal for supplies. He says:

I feel that the people of Beloit and its vicinity would consider it a pleasure to afford comforts to the soldiers, and especially to the soldiers from their own place. Many of our boys have but one blanket, and that single, and have received no overcoats, and consequently suffer from the cold. We have received no pay and the men have no way of making themselves comfortable. [62]

This letter must have brought a pang to the women of Beloit, who had worked so hard to make their boys comfortable, and it showed them also that better and securer means of transportation were needed for the supplies which were forwarded by the aid societies.

On Thanksgiving Day, 1861, the men of Company I of the Sixth Wisconsin Regiment were made very happy, for express wagons came to camp loaded with remembrances

---

[60] *Id.*, i, p. 281.
[61] *Ibid*, p. 59.
[62] *Id.*, ii, p. 78.

SOLDIERS' AID SOCIETIES

from home; and what could be more delightful than a bundle from mother, sister, or one still as dear, the girl he left behind him. In the boxes were "some stockings with the double heels and well-rounded toes, that mother carded, dyed, and spun, and sister knitted; some blue and white and red striped mittens with a place for the index finger. * * * Too much mince-pie and doughnuts caused some weak stomachs to ache, which was pronounced malaria, and remedied with the world's favorite prescription, quinine." [63]

About this time a soldier of the Eighth Regiment wrote: "If you have any old clothes lying around your sanctum, that will hold together in coming to us, send them; and if you have any patriotic old ladies in your part of the country, for peace's sake and the Union, set them to knitting stockings"—an appeal which probably stirred the patriotic women to whom it was addressed.

Contributions for Local Companies

During the early part of the year 1862, almost every box sent out from Wisconsin societies was designed for some specific military organization, and much delicacy was required on the part of the Sanitary Commission to temper the inevitable disappointment arising from the discovery that such stores could not always be forwarded by them to the designated address. [64]

Probably individual boxes continued to go to Wisconsin soldiers throughout the war, although less mention is made of them in the letters written in 1863 and 1864. Boxes

---
[63] Earl M. Rogers, in Viroqua *Leader* (Nov. 21, 1906).
[64] Henshaw, p. 35.

WISCONSIN WOMEN IN THE WAR

for local companies also became less frequent, partly because they so often failed to reach their destination, and partly because the supplies were sent in care of the Sanitary Commission.

A step in the direction of general supplies was taken in 1862, when the Governor of Wisconsin called for contributions for Wisconsin soldiers, rather than for individuals or companies. This meant that the aid societies should in the future send boxes to Wisconsin soldiers whom they had perhaps never seen, instead of to their friends and neighbors; they afterwards came to see that all supplies should be sent to Union men, irrespective of state lines.

A Milwaukee Donation

After the battle of Pittsburg Landing, Governor Harvey called upon the women of Madison and Milwaukee for a supply of bandages and shirts to be sent with Surgeon-General Wolcott to Tennessee.[65] The response of Milwaukeeans was as spontaneous as it was generous. Circulars setting forth the matter were sent to every part of the city; and an appeal to the people was published in the daily *Wisconsin*. The result was that a swarm of people poured into the Chamber of Commerce with contributions.

> A more cheering sight we never witnessed. Nothing like it was ever known in the history of Milwaukee. Men, women, and children came out from their homes with bundles, baskets, boxes, arms full and wagons full of valuable material, necessary articles, luxuries, and conveniences of various kinds—all of which will be needed, and will do some poor suffering soldier the good

---

[65] E. B. Quiner, *Military History of Wisconsin* (Chicago, 1866), pp. 211, 212.

SOLDIERS' AID SOCIETIES

for which it was intended, when it reaches its place of destination. Some took large bundles, supplied with goods, fresh from the stores, from their wardrobes, their tables, etc., articles which had never been used. Among these were even new table-cloths, that had never been spread upon the table, new towels, and a splendid collection of preserved fruits.

But the simple offerings of the poor were none the less acceptable, although they may not be of so much use. These were the offerings of mothers, who have sent sons to the war, of sisters, who have sent brothers to the field, and many others in similar circumstances, who, although they were not able to give as liberally as others, yet the life-blood of their friends has perhaps been offered up * * * and the small donations, which they presented last night, were as cheerfully received as the richest, because they came from the heart and were an earnest of what they would do, if they could. [66]

There was one old lady, who went to the Chamber of Commerce from the outskirts of the city, with a small bundle of linen handkerchiefs, which had been worn, but her mite gave evidence of her will, had she had the ability to do better. Another old lady took a muslin skirt. She had nothing else she could give—and it was much for her. One little boy took some small volumes of books that had whiled away the hours of sick persons in his own home. [67]

We heard of one lady, who was called upon by a neighbor, and asked to give something to send away, when she replied that really she didn't know what to send. "But stop a minute," said she, "here's something you might as well have," and she took six new shirts belonging to her husband out of the drawer and handed them over. On being expostulated with for sending new ones she said, "Oh! well, I can make more for my husband at any time, while the soldiers want them now." The lady was in good circumstances and could afford it, but doubtless many and many an instance of this kind took place, where it could not be

[66] *Corres. Wis. Volunteers*, vi, p. 51.
[67] *Ibid*, p. 52.

WISCONSIN WOMEN IN THE WAR

so well afforded, if the facts were all known. Such was the spirit that manifested itself yesterday.

Some sent boxes, some nails (these were useful for packing the goods), some entire pieces of sheeting, some sides of sole-leather (useful for splints), some wines, some magazines, and all descriptions of goods and luxuries were sent in. Wealthy citizens, who would never at any other time be seen with a bundle in their possession, now went to the rooms with their arms full of articles rolled up for the wounded soldiers. Ladies took their offerings often with their own hands, and sometimes having servants with them to carry the ponderous bundles and heavy baskets. [68]

By ten o'clock that night enough goods had been received and packed to fill about forty dry-goods boxes, and in addition the patriotic ladies, who formed an association for sending supplies to wounded soldiers, sent also some additional boxes.

The committee estimated that as a result of this remarkable manifestation, about ten thousand dollars worth of supplies had been contributed, which were sent directly to Pittsburg Landing, where Governor Harvey and a special committee were to distribute them. [69]

Aid Societies Discouraged

Between July 1862 and July 1863, there was every reason for the women of the North to be discouraged. The whole North was appalled by the defeats sustained by the Union army; Vicksburg had not been captured, the Mississippi was still unopened, Missouri and Kentucky had been invaded, and Maryland and Pennsylvania had been raided;

---

[68] *Ibid*, p, 52.
[69] *Ibid*, p. 52.

SOLDIERS' AID SOCIETIES

and the reports of the disastrous battles fought around Richmond were most discouraging—these almost paralyzed the activity of the Northern women, who simultaneously were informed that supplies, both private and public, did not reach their destination. Added to these calamities were the systematic assaults on the Sanitary Commission by the opponents of the administration.[70]

Such letters as the following could not have had a very cheerful effect upon the women. The writer says:

> I must not forget to acknowledge the non-reception of that box of good things, which I am informed the ladies have started down this way for us. We feel grateful to the fullness of our souls for such a demonstration of remembrance, and although we have not received it and do not expect to, yet we appreciate such kindness toward us all the same.

Even more doleful is the tone of another communication:

> At the time your Soldiers' Aid Society sent a box of things to St. Louis, soldiers from Racine lay sick in the hospital at Ironton, a branch of the St. Louis concern, and had not their company officers literally forced the managers of the hospital to admit their comrades to take care of them, these sick men would have died from sheer neglect. How much good has the Soldiers' Aid Society of Racine done these volunteers from Racine?[71]

This letter must have aroused much impotent anger and sorrow in the breasts of the loyal women of Racine, all the more on account of the apparent hopelessness of mending the situation.

The climax was reached, however, in the following sarcastic remarks:

> But the grand hoax is with the females and societies. The

---
[70] Henshaw, p. 75.
[71] *Corres. Wis. Volunteers*, ii, p. 26.

dear creatures exert themselves to send some luxury to wounded or sick soldiers that have left home, friends, and comforts of almost every kind. * * * But very few privates ever get a smell of any article they send, unless by an agent. Well, you will ask why? I will tell you. In the first place the officer of the post has the first taste, and then it goes through the hands of doctors, stewards, cooks, and ward-masters, and all have a taste; also their friends, and if the plate ever gets to the sick room, which it seldom does, it is empty; and I hope the supply will be stopped. Give what you have to give to the poor among you, but do not let your charities be so basely misapplied. [72]

After such attacks as this, many of the aid societies became irresolute and disheartened, and a few even ceased to work. The Commission received a great number of complaints, requests for explanation, and letters of protest. The following communication is typical:

I am called upon by the women of our town to say to you, that they wish to contribute to the sick and wounded, if they can. But sick soldiers and wives who have returned with their wounded husbands, tell us, that the sick *do* not and *will* not get the things we send them.

At a regular meeting during this period it was actually discussed whether the Sanitary Commission ought not to be discontinued. "If we are really of no use, what is the use of continuing our labors?" said one of the workers. But there was a fearful increase of sickness in the Western armies, and there were still many loyal aid societies who continued the work. Moreover, when they understood the situation, they realized that single packages or boxes could not be accounted for, because the things they contained

---

[72] *Ibid*, p 205.

SOLDIERS' AID SOCIETIES

were repacked at Chicago, and sent in different boxes, to different parts of the army.[73]

The National Spirit Grows

The Northwest was remote from the rest of the nation, and much time elapsed before the national aid idea penetrated our section. As late as 1863, societies wished occasionally to benefit their own regiments, which the Sanitary Commission also allowed in some few cases. At one time the members of a Wisconsin delegation, eager to help certain Wisconsin soldiers, obtained access to a certain hospital in the Army of the Cumberland. After a short time, they realized their selfishness in bestowing their gifts upon a few, wherefore they dropped their original plan and included all the patients in their ministrations. One Wisconsin soldier, who appreciated this change, said: "I am glad that they gave to the rest of the soldiers; it made me feel bad yesterday when the Ohio boy in the next cot got nothing, and I had so much; but when they were gone, I made it even."[74]

It may be considered, that there were three stages in the work of the Wisconsin aid societies—the first, the period of individualism; the second that of State aid, regardless of local interests; and the third the period of aid to the nation. It must not be supposed, however, that this progress was systematic and continuous, for individual and local boxes were sent throughout the war, and the stage of national relief did not preclude that of State relief. By the summer of 1863, however, Wisconsin women had arrived at Fred-

---

[73] Henshaw, pp. 75, 80.
[74] *Ibid*, pp. 108, 109.

WISCONSIN WOMEN IN THE WAR

erick Law Olmstead's conclusion, "It is, to say the least, a higher form of benevolence and of patriotism, which asks only to have a reasonable assurance that the soldiers of the Union will be helped by our offerings when and where they must need our help, and it is only by the exercise of this larger benevolence, that measures of relief can be taken at all adequate to the necessities of the army, or commensurate with the grandeur of its purposes." [75]

This thought was also expressed by Mrs. Teale of Allen's Grove, who said: "In the light of war, I view every loyal soldier as my brother." [76]

There were several reasons for the changed attitude of Wisconsin women by July, 1863. As has been stated, boxes which were sent directly to individuals, failed often to reach their destination, and the aid societies had finally become convinced that the only sure method of reaching the front was through the Commission. They had also learned, that supplies sent through the Commission really reached the army, for many of them had adopted the expedient of pinning notes requesting replies, in the pockets of dressing gowns, to shirt-bosoms, in the toes of socks, or in any other places where the soldier, who received the article, would be likely to find the message. And when they began to receive responses to their notes, they realized that the Union soldiers were really profiting by their exertions. Moreover, they were reassured when agents were sent to the South to find out what actually became of their sanitary supplies. Most important of all was a change of feel-

---

[75] U. S. Sanitary Commission *Documents* (New York, 1866), No. 50.

[76] *Corres. Wis. Volunteers*, v, p. 270.

ing, which spread rapidly over the North; the "first flush of hope and the reaction of disappointment had passed, and the people addressed themselves firmly and steadily to the task of saving the country."[77] New aid societies were formed, and the old ones stimulated to renew their efforts, even after such defeats as those at Fredericksburg and Chancellorsville.

Another cause of the renewed life in the aid societies was the energy of the Commission itself. In sheer desperation it had finally appealed to the churches and especially to the ministers in the Northwest, who did a remarkable work in stirring up patriotism, and in encouraging the formation of new aid societies. Moreover, the stirring appeals of Mrs. Hoge and Mrs. Livermore aroused Wisconsin women to new exertions.

So the Wisconsin societies began anew to work for the Commission, and contributions poured into the Chicago Branch "like a Western freshet." From four boxes a day in December, 1862, the number increased to 100 boxes a day in February, 1863.[78] From 250 aid societies connected with the Chicago Branch, the number increased to 1,000; so that by the summer of 1863, the Commission had entered upon the most prosperous period of its existence, and Wisconsin women were straining every nerve to do their share.

Difficulties Surmounted

What the societies of Wisconsin accomplished was all the more remarkable, when the difficulties under which they

---

[77] Henshaw, p. 75.
[78] *Ibid*, p. 102.

WISCONSIN WOMEN IN THE WAR

worked are considered. Throughout the war Wisconsin labored under disadvantages due to the sparseness of her settlement. She was poor, compared with the Eastern states, and time given to such charitable purposes meant money; for if women attended aid societies, they could do less in their homes.

That the societies were often destitute of funds, and almost heroic in raising them, the following letter from a woman in Melrose shows:

> We have not an average attendance of more than six. To raise funds to work with, we went around, and solicited donations of wheat from the farmers. We sent it eighteen miles to market, sold it, and bought materials. Though our offering is small, we hope it will do some good. [79]

As the war went on, housekeepers drew more and more upon their own supplies, especially in the country. The cellar was again and again invaded, and family stores, whether of bedding or clothing, were called into requisition. [80] In one case the wife of a minister stripped her beds so bare for the soldiers, that her husband was forced to appeal to the good women of the church for a cover for the night. [81]

Scurvy Combatted

Another line of aid society work grew up in the spring of 1863; namely, the sending of vegetables to the army as "anti-scorbutics" or preventatives of scurvy—a dreadful disease, caused by a lack of fresh fruit and vegetables. On

---

[79] Letter of Mrs. H. A. Pollis, in Henshaw, p. 125.
[80] *Ibid*, p. 125.
[81] Ms. letter of Miss Simmons.

SOLDIERS' AID SOCIETIES

March 4, 1863, the Chicago Branch issued an appeal to the Northwest for vegetables for Grant's army. The short, but urgent circular read, "General Grant's army in danger of scurvy. Rush forward anti-scorbutics." This message was sent to Milwaukee, Beloit, Madison, Racine, Sheboygan, Whitewater, and other towns, and the response was characteristic of the spirit of Wisconsin women. Although it was March, the weather rainy, and the roads very muddy, committees went abroad wherever telegrams were received or newspapers read, begging anti-scorbutics for the soldiers.

The movement was well organized; towns were divided into districts, every house was visited, and a central depot of supplies established. In the country these committees drove round in wagons, begged as they went from house to house, and took with them what was given. This was done day after day, first in one direction, then in another, through mud and rain, by men and women of all classes. Delicate women who could scarcely endure exposure, farmers' wives who could ill afford the time, tradesmen, and even clergymen went out on this generous mission. To remarks which were made, deprecating such effort, the answer was, "Our soldiers do not stop for the weather; neither must we." [82]

A fearful drought during the preceding summer, and a rot caused by the following wet winter, had greatly affected the supply of vegetables. In Illinois and Michigan there was a great dearth of them, but Wisconsin and Iowa were fortunately better off. So whatever supply there was in a

---

[82] Henshaw, p. 118.

home, was cheerfully divided with the soldiers.[83] In quantities, descending from bushels to pecks, from pecks to quarts, from quarts to handfuls, the precious stores were gathered. Pickles were brought out, cabbage pits opened and rifled, horseradish was dug up and forwarded.

Consignments were rushed to Chicago from Wisconsin, which filled the depot, overflowed on to the sidewalks, and even encroached upon the street in front of the Commission rooms. As fast as the vegetables arrived, they were sent South, and their places taken by other consignments. Milwaukee, West Milwaukee, Racine, and Whitewater were especially energetic, and hurried on carload after carload of precious, homely vegetables; a few farmers from Windsor, Bristol, and Spring Prairie forwarded 228 bushels.[84]

The activity of the aid societies was astonishing. Besides the regular meetings, extra ones were called. The neighborhood was canvassed, and the begging-committee was ordered to report on certain days, when the members of the society gathered, anxious to hear the result. Whoever was present, was courteously asked to assist in preparing the sauerkraut and the horseradish, and in packing and forwarding these articles, as well as onions and potatoes.[85]

The reunions of the aid societies were turned into pickling meetings. Barrels and kegs were begged and purchased, sauerkraut cutters were borrowed or hired, and men were employed to use them in cutting the cabbage to

---

[83] *Ibid*, p. 118.
[84] *Ibid*, p. 120.
[85] *Ibid*, p. 121.

SOLDIERS' AID SOCIETIES

the requisite fineness; then aids packed it with layers of salt, and poured vinegar over the whole. Grating committees, amid much rallying, and with many tears, courageously attended to the horseradish.

Soon a "line of vegetables" connected Chicago and Vicksburg, maintained by the shipment of a hundred barrels a day. [86] The importance of this movement on the part of the loyal women can hardly be overestimated, as it was an emergency which the Government could not have successfully met without the aid of the Sanitary Commission. This movement did more to establish its reputation for usefulness, than all previous efforts in other directions. [87]

It was not only Grant's army that was threatened with scurvy, but also the Army of the Cumberland, and there is no doubt that the fresh vegetables and dried fruit sent from the North acted as a successful preventive. But the disease was not yet conquered; in April, 1864, another call was made for anti-scorbutics, and again the rooms of the Chicago Commission were inundated with vegetables; the shipments from Wisconsin were so great, that a special mention of the Wisconsin aid societies was made in Mrs. Livermore's communication of July, 1864. [88]

Not only vegetables came in numbers, but "rivers of blackberry-juice" flowed in from all parts of the country; the supply was not sufficient, however, and a call was therefore again issued for dried fruits of all sorts. The circular reads: "The army is leading the same life, eating the

---

[86] *Ibid*, p. 121.
[87] *Sanitary Reporter* (published by the U. S. Sanitary Commission, Louisville), Nov. 1, 1863.
[88] Henshaw, p. 234.

WISCONSIN WOMEN IN THE WAR

same food, and incurring the same risks."[89] The Commission goes on to express its strong disapproval of canned fruit, and gives directions for drying peaches by dividing them into halves, and placing them on sloping boards in the sun or in slightly-heated ovens; this was such a simple task, that even children were urged to do it. The latter were also asked to have little gardens, where they could raise fresh vegetables for the soldiers. The whole crusade against scurvy shows the efficiency of the Commission machinery, as well as the splendid generosity and enterprise of the women of the Northwest.

Amount Contributed

So far, concrete instances have been given of the helpfulness of Wisconsin's women; a few statistics will give a better idea of the amount of work actually accomplished. In September, 1863, Wisconsin societies sent 110 packages from Milwaukee, Prairie du Chien, Watertown, Appleton, Beloit, etc. Compared with the other Northwestern states, namely, Illinois, Michigan, and Iowa, Wisconsin was number four on the list. In October packages came from Hartford, East Delavan, Green Bay, Madison, Oshkosh, Sheboygan, and Watertown. The whole number of packages was now 201, and Wisconsin was number three on the list. By November Elkhorn, Fox Lake, Hazel Green, Salem, and other towns were sending large contributions, and as a result Wisconsin headed the list with 510 packages. In December the number of packages had dropped to 301, but Wisconsin was still in the lead, a most remarkable fact, con-

---

[89] U. S. Sanitary Commission *Bulletin*, Sept. 15, 1864.

SOLDIERS' AID SOCIETIES

sidering the State was but fifteen years old and had a small population.[90]

Not only packages, but money was sent from Wisconsin to the Chicago Branch of the Commission. The money came from individuals, from aid societies, and from church collections, especially those taken at Thanksgiving time. The largest contributions of money and packages came from the Milwaukee Branch. None of the amounts exceeded one hundred dollars, and many of them were small; but poor communities did their best, and showed their kind spirit in forwarding as much as they could afford.

The aid societies contributed more generously in 1864 than the year before. In March the number of packages received by the Chicago Branch was 2,314. Of this number Wisconsin sent 629 packages, more than any other state. In April the number from Wisconsin increased to 776 packages out of a total of 1,810, placing her again at the head of the list. Wisconsin furnished in May 416 packages out of 1,974, with only Iowa and Illinois surpassing her.[91]

Conditions were different in 1864 from those of the preceding years. Out of every $100,000 worth of sanitary supplies in 1862, $90,000 worth came from the people, without any cost to the Commission; but out of $100,000 worth of supplies in 1864, $80,000 worth had to be bought with ready money.[92] This was due to the fact that homes had become exhausted, and that people who contributed to the sanitary fairs felt less like going outside of their own

---

[90] Northwestern Sanitary Commission *Reports*, Sept.–Dec., 1863.
[91] *Id.*, March to June, 1864.
[92] *Id.*, May and June, 1864, p. 21.

[47]

WISCONSIN WOMEN IN THE WAR

homes to buy the articles desired. Since sanitary supplies were needed as much at this time as earlier, it is gratifying to know that Wisconsin responded so well to the appeal of the Commission.

Summing up the work of the Northwestern states, we find that Wisconsin was the second on the list with regard to the number of packages contributed; and third in money contributions. She sent 8,896 packages, while Illinois surpassed her with 12,112. In money our State contributed during the four years of the War, $10,958.64. [93]

---

[93] Henshaw, p. 314.

Chapter III

The Wisconsin Soldiers' Aid Society, and Mrs. Henrietta Colt

The Milwaukee Branch had so remarkable a history and such an efficient secretary that it has seemed best to give it a chapter to itself. On April 19, 1861, a large number of Milwaukee women assembled in a school-room for the purpose of organization. They had been much agitated over the reports from the South, concerning illness among Wisconsin soldiers, and the need for post and general hospitals. Mrs. Margaret Jackson of Louisville, Kentucky, and Mrs. Louisa Delafield had awakened much interest in such matters.[94] At this meeting was organized the Ladies' Association of Milwaukee, with the following officers: President, Mrs. C. A. Riehr; Vice-Presidents, Mrs. Delafield. Mrs. McClure, Mrs. Jackson, and Mrs. Colt; Secretaries, Mrs. Ogden and Mrs. Dousman; Treasurer, Mrs. John Nazro.

Correspondence was opened with the surgeons of the regiments and with members of the Sanitary Commission, in order to gather such information as would enable the new organization to do its work intelligently. The first donations were sent to St. Louis, where many Wisconsin soldiers were efficiently cared for.

---

[94] L. P. Brockett and M. C. Vaughan, *Women's Work in the Civil War* (Boston, 1868), p. 607.

WISCONSIN WOMEN IN THE WAR

As time went on other Wisconsin societies wished to become auxiliary to the Milwaukee Branch, so the latter changed its name to the Wisconsin Aid Society,[95] and became a channel for Wisconsin benevolence. At the reorganization a notable woman, Mrs. Henrietta Colt, became corresponding secretary, and from this time on her public life is so interwoven with this society, that it becomes necessary to speak of her in more detail.

Like many Wisconsin women of her day, she had spent her younger days in New York state, where she had married Joseph S. Colt, a well-known lawyer of Albany. In 1853 they came to Milwaukee, where they remained for three years. At their expiration Mr. Colt returned East, where he died, leaving an honored name.[96] His widow and her family made their future home in Milwaukee.

Mrs. Colt was fitted by nature as well as by training to be a leader among women. Without being beautiful, she possessed an attractive personality, was a lady in the best and truest sense of this word, while her social graces were no less than the firmness, executive ability, and enthusiasm which characterized her mind. A writer who saw her in 1863 says:

I was much impressed with her intelligence, her purity of character, the beautiful blending of her religious and patriotic tendencies, the gentleness and tenderness with which she ministered to sick soldiers, and the spirit of dignity and humanity that marked her manners and conversation.[97]

---

[95] *Ibid*, p. 607.

[96] C. R. Tuttle, *Illustrated History of the State of Wisconsin* (Boston, 1875), p. 717.

[97] Brockett, p. 610.

THE WISCONSIN SOLDIERS' AID SOCIETY

A finer analysis of her character and public life is this: Into Mrs. Colt's public efforts was infused a species of mild audacity peculiarly her own. It was as though she had emerged from the retirement of private life under a sort of mental protest; as though she were nerved up to a conscious daring, and deprecated, yet defied criticism. There was in her letters to the Commission, during the earlier part of the war, a passionate ring, a pleading pathos, that revealed a nature in whose depths were concealed the noblest possibilities.[98]

Visits to Southern Hospitals

Mrs. Colt's most useful public work was done in the South, where she was sent in order to stimulate supplies at home by reporting what benefits were really conferred by the Sanitary Commission.[99] On January 5, 1863, an order was written by the president of the Chicago Sanitary Commission to the officers in command of the United States Army, giving Mrs. Hoge and Mrs. Colt the right to visit the hospitals and camps in and about Vicksburg and Memphis, to distribute supplies for the Chicago Sanitary Commission, and to "report to this Commission everything in regard to the need of sanitary stores, the kinds wanted, the best method of preparing and forwarding, and whatever else may be important or valuable for our Commission to know."[1]

Early in 1863 the two women left Chicago for Vicksburg with a large quantity of sanitary stores. Sherman had just been defeated, so there was much suffering in the army. The boat on which they travelled, was seized as a military

---

[98] Henshaw, p. 209.
[99] Brockett, p. 611.
[1] N. W. Sanitary Commission *Report*.

WISCONSIN WOMEN IN THE WAR

transport at Columbus, and pressed into the fleet of General Sherman. General Fisk's headquarters were on this same boat, and he gave the women every facility for carrying on their sanitary work. Their stores were practically the only ones on the fleet, which was composed of thirty ships, filled with fresh troops, whose ranks were soon thinned by illnesss. The boat became the refuge for the sick and wounded of Fisk's brigade, and the women nursed hundreds of men and saved many valuable lives. [2]

In March, 1863, Mrs. Colt went South again, this time with Mrs. Livermore and other members of the Sanitary Commission. They were to visit every hospital from Cairo to Young's Point, opposite Vicksburg, and their duties were to relieve the most pressing needs of the soldiers, to be useful to the sick, to cooperate with medical and military authorities, and to report the result of their observations in the Chicago papers and the bulletins of the Sanitary Commission. They had also with them stores necessary for sanitary relief, especially vegetables for patients threatened with scurvy. They carried 500 private boxes; and volunteered through the daily papers to take letters, messages, and small packages to army people on their route, and to deliver them, if possible. The sanitary stores were to be distributed among the matrons in the hospitals.[3]

Mrs. Colt visited also the Army of the Cumberland and saw every hospital soldier of the Wisconsin troops.[4] In speaking of these visits, she says:

I have visited seventy-two hospitals and would find it difficult

---

[2] Brockett, p. 568.
[3] Livermore, p. 282.
[4] Brockett, p. 612.

THE WISCONSIN SOLDIERS' AID SOCIETY

to choose the most remarkable among the many heroisms I every day witnessed. I was more impressed by the gentleness and refinement that seemed to grow up in the men, when suffering from horrible wounds, than by anything else. It always seemed to me, that the sacredness of the cause for which they offered their lives, gave to them a heroism almost superhuman, and the sufferings caused an almost womanly refinement among the coarsest men. I have never heard a word or seen a look, that was not respectful and grateful.[5]

Again she says:

I saw 600 wounded men with gaping, horrible head and hip gun-shot wounds. * * * I could have imagined myself among men gathered on cots for some joyous occasion, all except one man, utterly disabled for life; not a regret, and even he thanked God devoutly, that, if his life must be given up then, it should be given for his country. After a little, as the thought of his wife and babies came to him, I saw a terrible struggle; the great beads of sweat, and the furrowed brow were more painful than the bodily suffering. But when he saw the look and heard the passage, "He doeth all things well," whispered to him, he became calm and said, "He knows best, my wife and children will be in His care, and I am content."[6]

Concerning the Memphis hospitals she declared:

Among the beardless boys it was all heroism. They gained the victory, they lost a leg there, they lost an arm, and Arkansas Post was taken; they were proud to have helped in the cause. It enabled them, apparently with little effort, to remember the great, the holy cause and give leg, arm, and even life cheerfully for its defense. I know now that love of country is the strongest love, next to love of God, given to man.[7]

---

[5] Tuttle, p. 717.
[6] Brockett, p. 612.
[7] *Ibid*, p. 612.

WISCONSIN WOMEN IN THE WAR

After her return from the South, Mrs. Colt spoke to many aid societies in different parts of Wisconsin; wherever she appeared, renewed interest and enthusiasm ensued.

Milwaukee Society Enlarged

Meanwhile the Milwaukee society broadened its scope, until it included several departments. Its first purpose was to forward supplies, but it also assisted soldiers' families to get payments from the State; secured employment for soldiers' wives and mothers, through contracts with the Government; found employment for partially disabled soldiers, and provided for widows and orphans.[8]

Early in its history, its officers decided to send supplies through the Chicago and St. Louis commissions, but so well were the contents of the boxes assorted and packed at Milwaukee, that they were sent straight to the front, without being inspected by the Chicago Branch. As Alfred Bloor says: "Not an article is repacked for transmission to Chicago and the front, which has not been put into perfect order, nor a potato rebarrelled, which has not had its evil eye eradicated, nor an onion that is not hard and sound peeled in the pickling-room."[9]

Between 1861 and 1865 the Milwaukee Branch received about fifty boxes from each of the following towns: Appleton, Almond, Berlin, Beloit, Baraboo, Columbus, Delavan, Fox Lake, Green Bay, Janesville, Kenosha, Milwaukee, Mazomanie, Oak Creek, Prairie du Sac, Portage, Port

---

[8] Love, pp. 1050, 1051.
[9] U. S. Sanitary Commission *Bulletin*. iii, p. 909.

THE WISCONSIN SOLDIERS' AID SOCIETY

Washington, Ripon, and Wauwatosa.[10] It received during 1864, 2,142 boxes, containing such articles as shirts, sheets, pillows, pillow-cases, comforts, blankets, bedticks, wrappers, coats, vests, trousers, towels, handkerchiefs, socks, armrests, pads, cushions, bandages, canned fruits, dried fruits, groceries, butter, cheese, wine, eggs, pickles, vegetables, and a few books and magazines.

One of the valuable services rendered by the society was the sending of fruit to the army. After the battle of Resaca, they sent to every wounded man within reach, a fresh orange or lemon to ease the burning thirst which usually accompanies a wound.[11]

Chamber of Commerce

The supplies sent during 1864 amounted in value to about $25,000, and this from a commonwealth with no large cities and a population far from wealthy. In order to secure such results nine hundred circulars were sent to every part of the State. Money was also collected under the good management of Mrs. Colt. In March and April, 1864, between $5,000 to $6,000 was contributed to the Wisconsin Society, and a monthly subscription of $1,000 was promised by the Milwaukee Chamber of Commerce; this donation was to be paid regularly until the close of the war.[12]

This subscription was secured in large part through Mother Bickerdyke's[13] effort, who visited Milwaukee at the

---

[10] Mrs. J. S. Colt, in Wisconsin Soldiers' Aid Society *Report* (Milwaukee, 1863).

[11] *Ibid.*

[12] *Ibid.*

[13] A well-known army nurse.

WISCONSIN WOMEN IN THE WAR

request of Mrs. Hoge and Mrs. Livermore. The Aid Society had already asked the Chamber of Commerce for an appropriation for wounded soldiers, but the president stated that the last regiment sent out from Milwaukee had cost their organization so much, that it could not afford to make a contribution to the Aid Society. On the receipt of this reply Mrs. Bickerdyke made a most unexpected speech. She portrayed the life of a private soldier, his privations, his sufferings, and his patriotism. She contrasted this with the sordid love of gain which not only shrank from sacrifices, but even begrudged the pittance necessary to relieve the suffering of the men:

And you, merchants and rich men of Milwaukee, living at your ease, dressed in your broadcloth, knowing little of and caring less for the sufferings of these soldiers from hunger and thirst, from cold and nakedness, from sickness and wounds, from pain and death, all incurred that you may roll in wealth, and your houses and little ones be safe; you will refuse to give aid to these poor soldiers, because, forsooth, you gave a few dollars some time ago to fit out a regiment. Shame on you. You are not men—you are cowards—go over to Canada—this country has no place for such creatures! [14]

After this impassioned philippic the Chamber of Commerce reconsidered its act, and made the appropriation.

Generous Contributions

Not only were supplies sent to Chicago and St. Louis, but generous contributions were sent to Camp Reno, Camp Washburn, and the Harvey Hospital at Madison. A summary of the amounts received and disbursed shows that

---
[14] Brockett, p. 178.

THE WISCONSIN SOLDIERS' AID SOCIETY

between October 19, 1861, and December 1, 1865, $23,000 were received from Milwaukee citizens and $5,000 from other parts of the State. If the contract for Government clothing is added to these sums, about $30,000 were received, and disbursed as follows: material for clothing, pickles, etc., $17,813; sent St. Louis Sanitary Commission $200, and Chicago Commission $2,410; $455 was paid to Mrs. Bickerdyke; $250 to the Harvey Hospital; while the sum of $5,067.90 was paid over to soldiers' wives and widows, and sick and wounded soldiers.[15]

Mrs. Colt says of the work of this department: "We are proud that Wisconsin, without the excitement of a fair, and remote from the seat of Government, has done her work so well." She states also, that the gifts from Wisconsin people during the war amounted to $200,000, and that the whole number of packages sent to soldiers was 6,000. Beyond a doubt the Wisconsin Aid Society was, next to the Chicago Branch, the strongest organization of its kind in the Northwest.[16]

Work for Soldiers' Wives

From a social and economic point of view the industrial aid department was most interesting, for it grew up in response to a very strong demand—namely, that of the mothers, wives, and children of the soldiers for aid and financial assistance.

Mrs. Colt went to Washington and appealed to the quartermaster-general for a share of army clothing, to be made up by soldiers' families. She succeeded so well, that ma-

---
[15] Wis. Aid Society *Report*.
[16] Frank Moore, *Women of the War* (Hartford, 1867), p. 581.

WISCONSIN WOMEN IN THE WAR

terial for twelve thousand garments was secured. By such methods as this, the industrial aid department was enabled to do its work, without taking a dollar from any soldiers' aid society.[17]

The officers of this department were: President, Mrs. William Jackson; Vice-President, Mrs. C. V. Kelley; Treaurer, Miss Lottie Ilsley. Under their energetic administration the work went swiftly forward, and the Government clothing was soon given out. This was done with great discrimination; widows and women having large families of small children, were always given the preference. Soon four hundred and seventy-five women were set to work, and the members of the society were kept busy cutting, folding, giving out, and inspecting from eight hundred to eleven hundred garments each week. But they gave their time and services willingly, upheld by the thought that these wives and mothers of soldiers were encouraged to work for themselves, and were saved from the humiliation of receiving charity.

In addition to the contract received from the general Government, the society applied to the State quartermaster-general at Madison for clothing to be made, and through this channel material for 1,904 pairs of army trousers was secured. It was really gratifying to find how large a number of women were capable of making these articles well; it was said of all the contracts, that the work was done in a very creditable manner. Fortunately the society through the kindness of the Milwaukee & Prairie du Chien Railroad secured free transportation from Milwaukee to Madison for the weekly transfer.

---

[17] Wis. Aid Society *Report*.

THE WISCONSIN SOLDIERS' AID SOCIETY

A letter written by Alfred Bloor, a member of the Sanitary Commission, contains an appreciation of the work done by Mrs. Colt. He says therein:

In the midst of the elect ladies sits the one, who not only gives all her days and sometimes sleepless nights to the Wisconsin Society, but, who two or three months ago, braving railroad smashes, Mosby's guerrillas, and all other perils of the road, journeyed all alone to Washington, and by her Napoleonic tactics so softened the hearts of stern officials of the Quartermaster's department—no, for it is too serious a matter for jesting—by her graphic representation of these very women now before me, soldiers' wives and widows, waiting for back pay or pension, through months and sometimes for over a year with the "hope deferred that maketh the heart sick"—waiting on such days as this, with hungry children cowering around her fireless hearth; by the power of truth and her pathetic delineations of the alternative if the boon were refused * * * obtained a Government contract for the making up of soldiers' underclothes, and it is by the work and pay afforded them, in sewing these clothes, that these poor women get the tea to soften their bread, and the salt and flour to flavor their children's potatoes.

Another important phase of the work of this department, was obtaining the money allowed by the laws of Wisconsin to the families of soldiers in the field, but which most of them were helpless to get for themselves; thus they often fell into the hands of interested persons, or still worse, became prey to sharpers who devour widows' houses, and afflict the fatherless child. Mr. Bloor continues his letter as follows:

In this room is a branch bureau of the great and beneficient Special Relief System of the Commission, and it has been organized by and is carried on under the instruction of the Secretary of State for Wisconsin. * * * Over this bureau presides the wife of an eminent judge * * * and on the table before her lie numerous blanks, which are rapidly being filled in by her-

WISCONSIN WOMEN IN THE WAR

self and her assistant. As fast as they are signed (or marked) by the claimants, they are laid together to be forwarded to Madison * * * for official action.

By her side lies a pile of bank checks, the fruit of former papers of the same kind, substantiating similar claims to payment of State dues. You should see how that poor German woman's square, heavy face, reddened by the frost and hardened by poverty and anxiety, refines and lightens up, as the stuff for the garment is put into her hands; or better still, the price of those she brings back, is handed to her to be exchanged for some little article of necessity, or to her luxury for herself or child. Or still better, as the pen is put into her fingers for the stiff, angular, black-letter-like German signature, that looks so hard and crabbed to English script-reading eyes, or is guided over the paper to form the cross, which indicates "her mark," which mark, simple as it is, is the "open sesame" to a Golconda of several greenbacks; or best of all, as the sundry dollars collected on a check in her favor are consigned to the depths of her glove, her handkerchief or her pocket. What a pity, she can't lay down her cross, once for all, when putting it on paper, and that she couldn't get a check cashed every week, without having to bear it. [18]

At the close of the war this department had funds enough to relieve widows with families of small children who had not yet received their pensions. One member of the board arranged an operatic entertainment, which realized three hundred dollars. This sum was used for the purchase of wood and provisions, and a fund for small loans. The only regret of these women was that they were unable to do more for the needy, and especially for the disabled soldier "who prefers staying with his family to receiving help elsewhere." [19]

---

[18] U. S. Sanitary Commission *Bulletin*, iii, p. 910.
[19] Wis. Aid Society *Report*.

Chapter IV

Conditions at Home

The maid who binds her warrior's sash
With smile that well her pain dissembles,
The while beneath her drooping lash
One starry tear-drop hangs and trembles,
Though Heaven alone records the tear,
And Fame shall never know her story,
Her heart has shed a drop as dear
As e'er bedewed the field of glory!

The wife who girds her husband's sword,
'Mid little ones who weep or wonder,
And bravely speaks the cheering word,
What though her heart be rent asunder,
Doomed nightly in her dreams to hear
The bolts of death around him rattle,
Hath shed as sacred blood as e'er
Was poured upon the field of battle!

The mother who conceals her grief
While to her breast her son she presses,
Then breathes a few brave words and brief,
Kissing the patriot brow she blesses,
With no one but her secret God
To know the pain that weighs upon her,
Sheds holy blood as e'er the sod
Received on Freedom's field of honor! [20]

---

[20] Thomas Buchanan Read, "Wagoner of the Alleghanies," in *Poetical Works* (Philadelphia, 1883), p. 257.

WISCONSIN WOMEN IN THE WAR

At the outbreak of the war, hard times set in throughout the North and continued until the autumn of 1862. Many families roasted dandelion-root with pure coffee, others used parched corn or rye as a substitute for coffee; brown sugar was used instead of white; in fact, luxuries did not appear on the table of the people during this period, and none were ashamed of their frugal repasts. The wearing of plain clothes became a fashion as well as a virtue. An opera was only occasionally heard, and theatre performances were few; amusements took on a character adapted to the existing conditions of life. A popular lecture, a concert, a church sociable with a charade relating to some striking event of the war, a gathering of young men and women to scrape lint for the wounded—these were the diversions from the overpowering anxiety weighing upon the people. [21]

Gaieties Checked

From July 1862 to July 1863, the whole North was cast into despondency by the reverses at Fredericksburg and Chancellorsville.

During that year social clubs ceased to meet. Men when they heard of a disaster would give up some festive entertainment, would forego even a quiet evening at cards. They had no disposition for mirth. Their hearts were with their dead and wounded fellow-citizens on the Southern battlefield; they sat in quiet and brooded over their country's reverses. No thoughtful American opened his morning paper without dreading to find that he had no longer a country to love and honor. [22]

---

[21] James Ford Rhodes, *History of the United States from 1850 to 1877* (New York, 1906), v, p. 190.
[22] *Ibid*, pp. 197, 198.

CONDITIONS AT HOME

If the men of the North were thus affected, the women who had sent their sons, husbands, or brothers to the front were even more saddened. In fact the heartrending anxiety and dreadful suspense, added to the fear of defeat, made the days gloomy and weary. Women waited with bated breath for the latest list of killed and wounded; they haunted the post-offices, and eagerly scanned the bulletin boards; and in the face of all this, they had to keep on with their work for the soldiers and the care of their families.

The wives and mothers of the common soldiers have had no annals written in books. Nevertheless to really understand and appreciate their patriotism and loyalty, the conditions under which they lived must be taken into consideration.

Provision for Volunteers' Families

When the soldiers marched away, they did so with the assurance that their families would be provided for in the following ways: In the first place, each private was to receive thirteen dollars a month and about fifty-two dollars in addition for his clothing. Such portion of his wages as he could save, would be sent to his family by means of allotment-commissioners, officials employed by the State for this purpose. The State of Wisconsin also gave additional money to the wives of volunteers, which amounted to five dollars a month with an additional sum of two dollars for each child. Besides these sums the citizens of some towns raised a fund for the families of the volunteers. Beloit secured $2,500; Platteville, $1,500; while Madison had a fund of $7,490 for that purpose. In several counties the

WISCONSIN WOMEN IN THE WAR

families of volunteers were provided for by means of a special tax, which in Green County amounted to $56,000. [23]

Destitution at Home

In certain towns wealthy citizens promised to see that no soldier's family should want for necessities of life. Had all these plans worked to perfection, the war-widows and their families would have been well taken care of, and less destitution would have occurred than did exist to a certain degree throughout the war. Among the causes for this sad condition the following may be cited. The volunteers were not paid on time, again and again soldiers complained that they had not received any pay for six months or longer.

Whilst sitting by his warm fire, well fed and well clad, does there never rise before him a sad picture of the hundreds of thousands of wives, mothers, and children left at home, entirely dependent for the absolute necessities of life on the monthly remittance of husbands and fathers now fighting our battles? Does he never realize the fact of the advanced prices of fuel and of food? Does he forget that many of the privates now in the army have left little homes behind them on which taxes are to be paid, and that those homes are now being sold for the payment of those taxes? I offer him pictures of little children, barefooted amongst the snows of * * * Wisconsin, of a half-clad mother's shivering, and without the means of purchasing fuel, over the body of her dying child. The hardships of a private's family are much greater than his in the field. [24]

This picture may be somewhat exaggerated perhaps; but the fact remains, that through the slowness of the Government to pay its defenders, much suffering was caused at

---

[23] Love, pp. 130, 136, 137.
[24] *Corres. Wis. Volunteers*, iii, p. 246.

CONDITIONS AT HOME

home that might otherwise have been avoided. The following serves very well as an illustration of governmental red-tape. Because the adjutant-general of Wisconsin failed to receive the reports of the Fourth Regiment for January, February, March, and April 1862,[25] the soldiers' families in Whitewater, Ripon, Sheboygan, Kilbourn City, Jefferson, Geneva, Hudson, Oconto, Sparta, and Chilton were during those four months compelled to get along without any assistance from their relatives in the field.[26]

It is not surprising that soldiers complained bitterly over the existing conditions. One of them wrote:

I candidly believe, that a large proportion of the sickness of our regiment is owing to the men not getting their pay, for many of our best soldiers have families at home, who are dependent on the husband, father, or son who is in the army for the necessaries of life, and as day after day, week after week goes by, and every mail brings urgent appeals from the dear ones at home for that assistance the soldier is powerless to give, he becomes disheartened, thinks if he were only home, how much better it would be; takes no interest in the drill, and soon gets homesick, and is good for nothing to himself or any one else, and then, if any slight indisposition steps in, imagines he is going to die, and in many cases does die, as I firmly believe, from diseases which he would never have contracted, had his mind been at ease about those who depended upon him for their daily bread. [27]

It might be supposed that the State money would have been paid regularly, but such was not always the case, for

---

[25] The reports for January and February seem to have been lost; those for March and April were not forwarded, through a misunderstanding.

[26] *Corres. Wis. Volunteers*, iii, p. 119.

[27] *Id.*, iv, p. 175

WISCONSIN WOMEN IN THE WAR

these payments were stopped between October, 1862 and February, 1863. The Legislature had passed an act, levying a direct tax of $275,000 State money, which could not be deposited in the treasury until the following February. Between November and February a sum of about $200,000 was needed to keep up the payments to soldiers' families. To provide for this amount the Senate passed an act authorizing the issue of bonds to the amount of $250,000; but the bill was defeated in the Assembly. A wrathful correspondent writes, "Mothers, when your children are suffering from want of food and comfortable clothing, remember whose action it was that deprived you of what was promised by the State, when you consented that your husband should leave his family to fight."[28]

Even the plan of raising bounties by county taxation was not uniformily successful. In December, 1861, the board of Richland County levied a tax of $2,500 to be used for the families of volunteers. But the soldiers from that county objected to the method proscribed. They felt that every family needed assistance, and that the larger should have a greater bounty than small ones, regardless of the amount paid into the treasury by each; while, according to the method of the board, some families received bounties, and others none at all. Moreover, before a woman could get a share of the money, she had to swear that she was a pauper. Much feeling was stirred up by this affair, and the county board probably got its just dues when the irate soldiers returned.[29]

---

[28] *Id.*, iii, p. 266.
[29] *Id.*, iv, p. 249.

CONDITIONS AT HOME

Promises Forgotten

The promises of wealthy men in many communities that the wives and families of soldiers at the front should be cared for, were not always redeemed. The following appeal shows how the volunteers felt about this matter:

Friends, please do not stand idle with your unsoiled hands folded and witness these ladies cut and haul their own wood, day after day and week after week, as you have already done, after urging their husbands to leave them in a state of utter helplessness, promising and that surely, to care for their wants; and also that you would furnish them with comfortable homes and wearing apparel. Please do your duty at home, if you are not on the bloody battle-field. [30]

The women of Lodi, from whom this complaint comes, had been criticized by the stay-at-homes for gadding among the men, whereupon an indignant soldier wrote:

Ah, how cruel! being forsaken by those who have promised to be their protectors, having to sally forth themselves to look after the humble pittance that Uncle Sam allows them to support their little flock, the heaven-daring, opprobious epithet falls upon their ears "gadding after the men." O Shame! where is thy blush? Let these epithets rest where they belong. [31]

Sometimes the soldiers themselves came to the aid of the destitute. A war-widow of Lodi, whose husband had died quite suddenly of fever, leaving a wife and five children, received a subscription from the members of Company A in order to keep her and the children from actual want. [32]

---

[30] *Id.*, i, p. 152.
[31] *Ibid*, p. 283.
[32] *Id.*, viii, p. 402.

WISCONSIN WOMEN IN THE WAR

But in spite of these various provisions there was destitution in many towns in the State, and measures were soon taken by philanthropic people to lessen it. At Madison especially effective work of this kind was done; there was great need for it, since Camp Randall was the most important military station in the State, and many soldiers' wives and families gathered there to bid their husbands or fathers goodbye. Most of these families came in from the surrounding country, many of them lacked either means or energy to get back to their homes, so it fell to the women of Madison to care for them. For this purpose a Ladies' Union League was formed, and through its efforts about 200 destitute families were clothed and fed. Their spiritual wants were also ministered to, for many of these women were like frightened children, needing to be soothed and comforted. Often the women of the League wrote for or read aloud letters to these women to keep up their hope and courage.

To get the necessary supplies for these families, committees were appointed to solicit from the Madison people, who responded most liberally. Some of the townspeople were so generous, that they stinted themselves in order to give to the destitute. Even the farmers from the neighboring country sent in pork, chickens, or butter to aid the cause. These gifts were received only occasionally, however, and by December, 1863, the League was in such straits for supplies that it decided to make a special appeal to the different sections of the surrounding country. Circulars were sent to the farmers inviting them to attend a great dinner in Madison, and to bring with them as many donations as possible. They responded nobly and brought great quantities of wood and vegetables of every kind, which the

CONDITIONS AT HOME

Madison grocers stored until they were needed. So great was the success of this party, that the society was lifted from its slough of despond, and enabled to care for its destitute families.

Philanthropic Spirit

Such philanthropic work was done in many places. In the small country towns women often made butter and sold it in order to obtain money for destitute families. Men gave also a helping hand to the war-widows by providing them with fuel, and helping their husbands to secure their back-pay. The whole State seems to have been full of this benevolent spirit, which manifested itself in many ways.

The spirit of humanity and brotherly love shown in the following story makes it worth narrating. Mrs. Isabel Leindecker was a young war-widow, whose husband had been reported missing in 1862. She had but five dollars left for herself and three children, and thought that if she could get her wood free, she might manage to get clothes and food for her children. So she concluded to have a wood bee. In vain her mother tried to discourage her, saying, "You will throw away your money." Nevertheless she invited twenty-five old friends and neighbors, but did not expect that all of them would come. Having delivered her invitations, she started to buy provisions for the expected guests; the first merchant whom she approached, shoved back her three dollars and a half, saying: "Take this, Isabel, as my share. The old man cannot come." At the meat market she met with the same kindness; the butcher said, that although he could not come, his two boys would help her to chop the fire-wood. As she passed the home of the butcher his wife brought out a bucket of ren-

WISCONSIN WOMEN IN THE WAR

dered lard, and on the morning of the bee one of his sons brought a large piece of salt meat, saying, "Isabel, the boys might like a piece of fried meat." Another friend brought her also a large piece of meat and a bucket of sauerkraut, together with a basket of eggs and butter from his wife. One friend sent a sack of potatoes and half a bushel of beets. The village blacksmith wished also to help; but since he had to sharpen the tools of the miners on Saturdays, he could not come, but he offered to cut wood at home on another day and promised to sharpen the tools which the men used, but, when he saw the many tools, he exclaimed: "Py kolly! I can't sharpen all doze in a week," and locking his shop, he fled to the woods.

Mrs. Leindecker's own story of the bee follows:

At eleven o'clock I sent my little brother to the woods to see how many were there. He soon came running back. "Oh Isabel! what will you do! There are forty men, and the trees are falling like grass." What did I do? Being only twenty-two years old, I sat down on the floor and cried like a baby. But not long did I sit there. I ran to the hotel kept by Mrs. Lafonte, and putting my hands on her shoulders I cried, "Mrs. Lafonte, how much have you cooked?" She answered, "Child, you shall have all I have cooked. and I will go to baking." * * * To make a long story short, only twelve men came to dinner, and six to supper; just enough to keep from hurting my feelings. To sum up the day's work, I had to my credit forty loads, nine hauled home and five chopped into stove wood, enough to last till the war was over. The very next week I received word from my husband, who had been a prisoner for eight weeks; I cried to think how much I had troubled the people, when after all my husband was alive to send me money.[33]

[33] Grant County Veterans' Association, Woman's Auxiliary, *Reminiscences of the Civil War* (Bloomington, 1902).

CONDITIONS AT HOME

The foregoing incident shows that in spite of the hardships of the time, in spite of high-prices and scarcity, there was a spirit of genuine sympathy and helpfulness among the men and women of Wisconsin.

Pathetic Incidents

Undoubtedly a certain amount of destitution had prevailed in Wisconsin before the war, but there can be no doubt that the war greatly increased the suffering. In small country towns there were many women left with large families, who found it exceedingly hard to get along. One woman, with twelve children, managed in some way without accepting charity. One of her children reports:

Of course some of us went out to work and helped all we could, but we did not get the wages girls do now and we had to work a great deal harder. I only got a dollar a week, and a dollar and a half was thought to be large pay in those days.

The mother of this girl had a hard time with only the two little boys at home to help her, for "they were small then and couldn't do much."

Another poor woman with nine children (the oldest only thirteen) almost starved to death, and instead of using her pig for food was compelled to sell it to pay her taxes. One brave little war-widow lived in a shanty, which cost forty-five dollars; it was built on a lot belonging to a citizen of the town. [34] Here she lived with her two children, keeping body and soul together by sewing for a woman in Manitowoc. With remarkable fortitude she bore her fate,

---

[34] Mrs. Fitzgerald, interviewed by author at Waupaca, March, 1910.

WISCONSIN WOMEN IN THE WAR

and still refuses to acknowledge that she underwent any real hardships during the war.

Sometimes the soldier, instead of being at the front, was at home sick. Mrs. H. had to support two children and a sick husband; the typhoid fever he suffered from, consumed every cent they had.

Perhaps the most pathetic case was that of Mrs. B., whose husband died in the South, leaving her with a sick child and no money. "There was twenty-five cents left after burying my husband," she said. But the plucky woman went to work in her father's home, where she alternately did house-work and carried the sick child in her arms. After waiting for four years she finally received her pension, which enabled her to build a small cottage at Waukesha.[35]

The case of Mrs. D. is worth recording. She was left with four small children and a homestead, which she was later compelled to mortgage. She managed to keep her home attractive; it was always bright and cheerful; her curtains were made from an old heliotrope dress; a drygoods box constituted her dresser, and her rug was braided from remnants of old trousers. The children's shoes were made from the tops of her old ones, her daughters wore combination dresses, while her boys wore trousers made of grain bags. Through sickness and poverty she preserved her cheerful disposition and managed to keep her family together, until her husband returned.[36]

---

[35] Mrs. Baker, interviewed by author at Waupaca, March, 1910.
[36] Mrs. Doty, interviewed by the author at Waupaca, March, 1910.

CONDITIONS AT HOME

Mrs. A. was left with seven children and a four hundred acre farm. Before her husband enlisted, he had borrowed six hundred dollars from a friend, who promised not to press him for the money, and to look after his family. Eight months after the husband's departure another child was born; thus the wife had eight small children to care for. In the meantime her husband had died in the South. Then her creditor insisted on the payment of the debt, and threatened to take the farm. She begged him to leave her enough land for a house and garden, but he refused, and the sheriff evicted her; her household goods were placed outside, and she was compelled to sit up all night, to keep the cattle from destroying her possessions. She managed to keep her family together; her children grew up to be useful and respected members of the community, but her terrible experience doubtless helped to shorten her life. [37]

High Prices

In cases such as these, the high prices demanded for the necessities of life without doubt increased the difficulties of living. Calico cost forty to fifty cents a yard, tea $2.00 a pound, kerosene sixty cents a gallon. Mrs. D.'s experience in buying goods is typical. She sold a piece of land for fifty dollars and went to town to make a few purchases. By the time she had finished her shopping, she had spent forty dollars; and the wash tub, in which she brought her purchases home, was only partly filled. Another warwidow states that "Flour was five dollars per hundred, so

---

[37] Ms. sent by Mrs. Martha Showalter (Lancaster, May, 1910).

WISCONSIN WOMEN IN THE WAR

we lived on corn-bread, and mush and milk, till I thought I should never like cornmeal again.''[38]

During this period many private fortunes were amassed; the minority seemed to fatten on the necessities of the majority. One indignant woman says:

> The sacrifices and hardships incident to war-widowhood were many, but they were borne cheerfully by all loyal women with the exception of those instances (and they were many) where the wives of the soldiers were the victims of extortion in the matter of the purchase of household supplies from heartless copperheads, who by short weight and short measure disposed of their commodities at a price not accordant with the market valuation. Sometimes the quality of the meat and vegetables that were sold by these human vampires to the war-widows, was so bad that it would not pass muster in a pigsty. * * * With heart and brain exercised to their fullest tension on account of friends who were in peril, and ill treatment by traitors at home, we had a generous measure of ills to bear.[39]

The Greater Sacrifice

As a rule, however, these women were philosophical. One of them writes:

> There was too much to be done by the most of us, to keep the wolf from the door, to give way to our feelings, and it was better so. It gave us the feeling that we, too, although not enlisted in the ranks South, had a battle to fight at home on more than one line, and the worst of all was to keep up hope against hope, that our loved ones would be spared to come back to us, no matter if they could only come; we would thank God,

---

[38] Mrs. Teresa Wilson, "A Memory of War Times," in Grant County Veterans' Association, Woman's Auxiliary, *Reminiscences of the Civil War*.

[39] Ms. sent by Mrs. H. J. Eldred (Waupaca, April, 1910).

CONDITIONS AT HOME

if they were only a shadow of what they were when they went away.

Probably the severest test of the patriotism of these women was when they were called upon to give up all hope of the return of sons, husbands, and brothers. Hardship and privation were nothing to endure compared with the loss in battle. A Kenosha woman had six brothers at the front; the seventh and youngest had remained at home to care for his aged parents; but he was also taken through the draft, and the parents were left alone. Four of these seven boys never returned, and today their sister is alone in the world.

The husband of a war-widow living near Tustin was captured at Ream's Station, Virginia, and sent to Salisbury Prison, North Carolina. Throughout the war he had kept in close touch with his wife and family, but after his imprisonment they received only one note. His wife was left in a fearful state of suspense regarding his fate, until she read in a Madison paper of his death.

Mrs. A. H. Hoge tells of a sad experience she had with a young Wisconsin soldier whom she met on board a hospital ship. He was an only child and a boy of rare promise; had been well educated, and was at the outbreak of the war ready to enter a law-partnership with his father. The day this young man left Wisconsin, his mother, forgetting all but her only child, threw her arms around the colonel of the regiment and said, "O, Colonel, for God's sake, guard my treasure, for he is my all." When Mrs. Hoge saw him, he was hopelessly ill, but did not realize that death was at hand. She said to him, "Suppose we never meet on earth again, what would you say." Looking up serenely,

WISCONSIN WOMEN IN THE WAR

he answered, "I understand you. Should I die, tell my mother that as I have lain here these weary days all her early teachings have come back, and I trust have done their work. * * * Tell her I never regretted the step I have taken. She must not mourn for me as without hope, for if I die, 'twill be in a glorious cause and our separation will be short." The next morning he was dead.[40]

A typical incident of its kind is the story told under the title, "One little mother."[41] She was a timid, gentle woman, but she possessed something of the soldierly spirit of her father; she did not complain, even when the last of her four brothers enlisted, and bade her goodbye. In the autumn of the same year she had a letter from her son in Dane County saying that he could not stay away from the army any longer. Though her heart had been strong she wept at the news, but the spirit of patriotism conquered her fears, and she wrote her boy a letter full of blessings, and bade him God-speed.

But this was not her last sacrifice; for in the summer of 1862 her fifteen-year-old son George, inspired by a war-meeting he had attended, decided to enlist. Again her love and her patriotism fought for supremacy, again patriotism conquered, and George enlisted. This left her with her husband, the baby, and her thirteeen-year old Herman. She prayed for the safety of her sons, and wrote to them such letters as only a mother can write. Even now the oldest son remembers the advice she gave him: "Try to keep your conversation among your comrades such that you

---
[40] Moore, pp. 356, 357.
[41] H. W. Rood, in Milwaukee *Sunday Telegraph*, March 6, 1887.

[76]

CONDITIONS AT HOME

would be always willing to have your mother hear it. * * * I beg you not to run any unnecessary risks, but your mother wants you, whatever may come, never to shirk from your duty." He says that the first piece of advice was much more difficult to follow than the second, but that he strove hard to live up to both, and that his mother's letters to him were a tower of strength.

Plenty of trouble came to this brave and noble woman. In 1862 one of her brothers died at Alexandria, Virginia, another was wounded that same year at Williamsburg, and came home with a ball in his ankle. Her eldest son was injured at Atlanta, but did not leave the army, re-enlisting in January, 1864. Her hardest experience was still to come, however; for when drafting began her husband was compelled to go, although his arm was so crippled that he could hardly handle a musket after reaching the front. To add to her anxiety, Herman, who was by that time sixteen years old, insisted on going to the front; thus she was left alone with her youngest son. Although the great loneliness oppressed her she wrote cheerful letters to her beloved ones; her neighbors were amazed that such a timid person as she could be so brave. Finally her reward came, for in August, 1865, her husband and two of her sons came back to Madison. They had planned to surprise the dear mother, so they came stealing into the room where she lay asleep and woke her by asking in a most matter of fact way for something to eat. When she opened her eyes she asked what the rascals meant by coming into people's houses and waking them up in the middle of the night. In her great joy she was the same composed, undemonstrative, and practical woman she had always been. The story is not unique

WISCONSIN WOMEN IN THE WAR

—there were many like her—but this serves to show the firmness of mind with which the loyal women of Wisconsin bore their trying experiences during the war period.

Women as Farmers

Perhaps the most striking phase of women's activity was their work on the farms. The importance of this army of workers cannot be overestimated, for without them agricultural production would in many cases have been stopped, although it must not be forgotten that the use of labor-saving machinery and the influx of new settlers were also factors in the maintenance of farm production throughout the war. Labor-saving machinery had been used before 1861, but its use became more common during the war period. At first mowers and reapers were utilized only on the largest farms; later their use was more general, and supplemented by that of the harrow, the grain-drill, the corn-planter, the steam-thresher, the revolving horse-rake, the rotary-spade, the steel plow, the thresher, and the two-horse cultivator.[42]

In many of the poorer communities, however, there was little or no labor-saving machinery and the women who did their own farm-work gathered in their crops in the old-fashioned way. The experience of Mrs. D. is a good illustration. In the part of the country where she lived, many of the women had no horses and were forced to har-

---

[42] E. D. Fite, *Social and Industrial Conditions During the Civil War* (New York, 1910), p. 6; "Agricultural Development of the West," in *Quarterly Journal of Economics*, xx, p. 271; R. G. Thwaites, "Cyrus Hall McCormick and the Reaper," in Wisconsin Historical Society *Proceedings*, 1908, p. 255.

WOMEN WORKING IN THE FIELDS, IN WAR-TIME

From sketch by Thomas Nast, in F. B. Goodrich, *The Tribute Book* (N. Y., 1865), p. 461

CONDITIONS AT HOME

ness oxen. She herself had to haul wood, and inexperienced as she was she broke the wagon-tongue in the process. Some of the women in her neighborhood sheared sheep, took the wool home, carded and spun it and made socks. Mrs. D. used to burn brush and build fences herself, and she also hoed and raked. She had once a trying experience with an unruly yoke of cattle, which used to get into the grain; often she had to get up in the middle of the night in order to drive them out. At one time she went to church, and returned to find fifteen of her neighbor's cattle in her wheat. She raised not only wheat, but also a little buckwheat; she hired a man to cut it, but threshed it herself. She had planted sixty bushels of sugar-cane on her farm and invited the soldiers in the neighborhood to a cutting bee; as a result she and the children lived well that winter on buckwheat and molasses. [43]

Such instances as the preceding were common in Waushara County, which had a poor and sandy soil and very little wealth. Many of the women in that county had patches which they cultivated with the help of children, for every able-bodied man had left for the front. A young girl went one beautiful afternoon out in the meadows to help her father. He did not want her to do a man's work; before the war, the women of his family only milked the cows and attended to the garden. He was an old man, however, and needed help, therefore he finally allowed his daughter to spread the hay; which occasion she afterwards declared was the proudest of her life.

Another woman living in Waushara County was left with only three old men to help her. They cut the wood,

---

[43] Mrs. Doty, interviewed by author at Waupaca, March, 1910.

WISCONSIN WOMEN IN THE WAR

she tended to the cows, cut hay with a scythe, and cradled and bound her oats.

Mrs. B. drove ten miles to Weyauwega to get wood to build a barn, hauled it back herself, and then shingled her barn.[44]

In some towns the women formed sewing-circles to make clothing for these women-farmers. They cut out and made children's garments as well as women's, and sold them as cheaply as possible to the women on the farms.

Occasionally women became agricultural laborers, but this was not common, for in many communities the people could not afford to pay for help. In a few places, however, German women hired out by the day and received good wages.

The number of women doing work on the farms increased as the war went on, because most able-bodied men were taken from their agricultural work and pressed into service in the army. Mrs. Livermore gives a vivid picture of her visit to Wisconsin and Iowa in the early summer of 1863, which shows to what extent women were then working on the farm:

> As we dashed along the railway, let our course lead in whatever direction it might, it took us through what seemed a continuous wheat-field. The yellow grain was waving everywhere; and two-horse reapers were cutting it down in a fashion that would have astonished Eastern farmers. * * * Women were in the field everywhere, driving the reapers, binding and shocking, and loading grain, until then an unusual sight. At first it displeased me, and I turned away in aversion. By-and-bye I observed how skilfully they drove the horses round and round the wheat field, diminishing more and more its periphery at every circuit,

---

[44] Mr. Eldred, interviewed by author at Waupaca, March, 1910.

CONDITIONS AT HOME

the glittering blades of the reaper cutting wide swathes with a rapid, clicking sound that was pleasant to hear. Then I saw, that where they followed the reapers, binding and shocking, although they did not keep up with the men, their work was done with more precision and nicety, and their sheaves had an artistic finish that those lacked made by men. So I said to myself, "They are worthy women and deserve praise; their husbands are probably too poor to hire help, and like the helpmeets God designed them to be, they have girt themselves to this work—and they are doing it superbly. Good wives! Good women!"

One day Mrs. Livermore drove twenty miles across the country, through the same "golden fields of grain and between great stretches of green waving corn." Some accident to her carriage caused her driver to halt opposite a field where six women and two men were harvesting. She walked over and accosted them:

"And so you are helping to gather the harvest!" I said to a woman of forty-five or fifty who sat on the reaper to drive, as she stopped her horses for a brief breathing spell.

"Yes ma'am," she said, "the men have all gone to the war, so that my man can't hire help at any price, and I told my girls we must turn to and give him a lift with the harvesting."

"You are not German? You are surely one of my own countrywomen—American?"

"Yes, ma'am; we moved here from Cattaraugus County, New York State, and we've done very well since we came. * * * It came very hard on us to let the boys go, but we felt we'd no right to hinder 'em. The country needed 'em more'n we. We've money enough to hire help, if it could be had; and my man don't like to have me and the girls a-working out doors; but there don't seem no help for it now."

I stepped over to where the girls were binding the fallen grain. They were fine, well-built lassies, with the honest eyes and firm mouth of the mother, brown like her and clad in the same sensible costume.

6 [81]

WISCONSIN WOMEN IN THE WAR

"I tell mother," said Annie, standing very erect with flashing eyes, "that as long as the country can't get along without grain, nor the army fight without food, we're serving the country just as much here in the harvest field as our boys are on the battlefield—and that sort o' takes the edge off from this business of doing men's work, you know."

Further conversation disclosed the fact that amid their double labor in the house and field, these women found time for the manufacture of hospital supplies, and had helped to fill box after box with shirts and drawers, dried apples and pickles, currant wine and blackberry jam, to be forwarded to the poor fellows languishing in far-off Southern hospitals. My eyes were unsealed. The women in the harvest field were invested with a new and heroic interest, and each hard-handed, brown, toiling woman was a heroine. [45]

A Prairie du Chien soldier writes:

There were four brothers of us, all single and all under age when we enlisted. This left two small brothers, three young sisters, and a father and mother to do the work of the farm. This meant planting and harvesting crops, cutting, curing, and stacking hay, fixing fences, chopping wood, caring for the stock, and in fact doing all the work that had been done before by the boys. These things my mother and sisters helped to do. This was the condition all through our section. From many families the husband enlisted, leaving the mother with small children. The mother and the small brood carried on all the work of the farm as they were able. They cleared land, chopped down trees, and clad in brown denim dresses they burned the brush and cultivated the soil. They gathered and marketed the crops and thus became not only self-sustaining, but actually had a surplus with which to help the nation. Two girls, whom I well knew, became as expert in harvesting grain and in chopping wood as any man in the country.[46]

---

[45] Livermore, pp. 144–149.
[46] Ms. letter of A. C. Wallin (Prairie du Chien, Feb., 1910).

CONDITIONS AT HOME

One women went from Madison into Columbia County, where she took up uncultivated land, which she broke herself; there she planted and raised crops and was thus able to support herself and her four small children. Her ambition was to make a home for her children, and for her husband if he ever returned; she knew that she might have been forced to accept charity if she had remained in Madison.[47]

Women in New Lines of Work

When the Civil War broke out the total number of women in Wisconsin was 367,000, of whom 17,500 were engaged in some occupation. The most popular, according to the number of women engaged in each pursuit, were: servants, 12,287; teachers, about 1,500; seamstresses, 1,191; milliners, 533; mantua-makers, 472; laundresses, 411; makers of men's clothing, 386; tailoresses, 208; housekeepers, 185; nurses, 184; and music teachers, 166.[48] The number of women engaged in manufacture was 773, apportioned as follows: men's clothing, 386; lumber (sawed), 79; millinery, 74; furniture and cabinets, 39.[49]

During the Civil War, Wisconsin women filled the places left vacant by the soldiers, so that by 1865 women had entered many fields of industry hitherto occupied by men only. Unfortunately there are no statistics for the latter

---

[47] Mrs. Bennett, interviewed by author at Madison, April, 1910.

[48] *U. S. Census*, 1860, vol. "Population." Women's occupations are only approximately by the compiler, for the census did not differentiate women from men, except in industrial lines.

[49] *Ibid*, vol. "Manufacturing," p. 658. Occupations omitted by compiler, where less than thirty women were engaged.

year, but it may be assumed that those for 1870 will approximately represent the conditions at the close of the war. In 1870 the number of women in Wisconsin was 509,000, of whom over 25,000 were engaged in the following occupations: servants, 15,879; teachers, 3,169; farmers, 1,387; mantua-makers, 2,132; seamtresses, 1,179; laundresses, 276; nurses, 67. The chief difference in the decade is that the number of women in commercial and industrial pursuits increased from 773 in 1860, to 3,967 in 1870. The statistics for 1870 are: men's clothing, 698; lumber (sawed), 362; woolen goods, 205; millinery, 155; furniture, 151; carpets, 116. Women are also recorded as workers in match factories, paper mills, straw-goods factories, cheese factories, book-binderies, and glove factories. Moreover, there were seventeen women keeping grocery stores in 1870; twenty-six selling or trading in agricultural implements; and ninety-two acting as clerks in stores. A few women are reported as peddlers, steamboat employees, bookkeepers, trunk and valise makers, dealers in books, stationery, and drugs, cigar makers, whip makers, fur dressers, in the manufacture of hoop-skirts, malt liquors, awnings, baskets, bags, curled-hair, etc. [50]

The census reports do not show that there was a great increase in the number of women employed; the percentage in 1860 is 4.4, while in 1870 it is 4.9; so that the main difference—aside from farm labor during the war, which does not appear in the census reports—lies in the greater diversity of occupations, particularly in industrial and commercial lines.

---

[50] *Id.*, 1870, vol. "Population and Social Statistics," pp. 666–690, 694, 695; vol. "Industry and Wealth," pp. 583, 584.

CONDITIONS AT HOME

From interviews and personal recollections a few more facts have been secured, relative to women's occupations. In Richland County one woman raised sage and sold it to the druggists of Richland County at a dollar a pound. Another occupation in that neighborhood was the digging of ginseng, which was sold to dealers and then shipped to China; in the ginseng season the woods were searched for it by scores of women. At Menasha in 1861 and 1862 a number of young women entered the factory of the Wooden Ware Company, in order that the men might enlist in the army.

Between 1861 and 1865 women's position among breadearners became more common, and by the close of the war they had invaded many new fields, not only in the industrial and commercial world, but also in clerical, charitable, and religious lines. [51]

The Sewing Machine

In the statistics given above it will be noticed that sewing was a favorite occupation for women in both 1860 and 1870. It is probable that the invention in 1849 of the sewing machine by Elias Howe, had much to do with making this occupation so popular. To make a man's shirt by hand required fourteen hours and twenty minutes steady work; with the sewing-machine, the same garment could be made in one hour and sixteen minutes. The popularity of the sewing-machine is shown by the fact that the number manufactured by the Wheeler and Wilson Machine Company, increased from 25,000 in 1860 to 40,000 in 1864; and

---

[51] Fite, p. 244 (note).

the number of Singer machines from 13,000 to 23,000.[52] Very few families in the small towns of Wisconsin possessed sewing-machines. A woman in one of these towns was very anxious to secure one, so in order to realize her desire she lived on bread and molasses for a long time, and tried to pay for a machine. A kind neighbor found out her plan, and she requested some of the members of her church to assist her. After securing the machine this woman made the clothing given her under the Government contract in a very short time. Probably without using the machine, neither she nor hundreds of others could have earned a living making these garments.

A Patriotic School Teacher

The increase in the number of women who taught school during this period is not at all surprising, since so many of these positions were left vacant by men who had gone to the front. The wages paid differed, however, for in 1860 a man received an average of $24.20 a month, while a woman received only $22.24. Very few accounts have been secured relating to the Wisonsin women who taught during this period. As an illustration of the patriotic spirit of one of these teachers the following story is told.

About nine miles from Waupaca a young woman taught a district school; she was devoted to the Union and taught her pupils to sing patriotic songs. The school board consisted mostly of Southern sympathizers, who told her that such songs would never do. The next day the children began their school work by singing "John Brown."

---

[52] *Ibid*, p. 89.

CONDITIONS AT HOME

That same morning the members of the board waited upon her, and informed her that she would have to choose between discontinuing the songs or closing the school. The plucky girl replied that she had a contract to teach, that the children were accustomed to sing in the morning, and should continue to do so.

On the third day following this episode, the teacher found the schoolhouse closed; but nothing daunted, she summoned the patriotic women of the neighborhood, who remained at the schoolhouse until noon as her witnesses. Her next act was to call on the school board and demand her salary for the whole period during which she had expected to teach. They refused to grant her request, but fortunately a company of soldiers had come home on a furlough and they insisted that justice be done. The case was at last carried to the circuit court, where the judge rendered a verdict in her favor. [53]

Confederate Prisoners

In the spring of 1862 the residents of Madison were much interested in the arrival at Camp Randall of a number of Confederates, who had been captured at Island Number Ten. A person present has described their coming:

A large crowd awaited their arrival, and when they came, regarded their removal from the cars to the camp, with curious interest. They were received by a guard of the Nineteenth Regiment, accompanied by a fife and drum band, playing lively airs. They passed between the files to the camp, many of them heavily laden with baggage. They all looked tired and jaded, and the pale faces of some of them showed that they were

---

[53] Mr. Eldred, interviewed by author at Waupaca, March, 1910.

WISCONSIN WOMEN IN THE WAR

seriously affected. When they were nearly inside the camp, the band struck up the tune of "Dixie" and the steps of the prisoners were at once made firmer and their eyes brighter. There were about sixty sick prisoners, and the removal of these afforded a painful spectacle. Its sadness was relieved, though, by the tender manner in which the soldiers of the Nineteenth supported their tottering steps, while helping them to the stretchers.

The prisoners cooked their own food, and seemed to be satisfied with the rations they received, although they missed the corn bread to which they had been accustomed. There was a prevailing anxiety among them for a supply of reading matter, and a few expressed a desire to work for the surrounding farmers, believing the work would be better for their health. From all accounts they were most humanely treated, and the spirit shown toward them by the residents of Madison was a generous and Christian one.

Madison women worked among these Confederate prisoners, especially in the hospitals, where they died like sheep. One woman, who did much toward making the prisoners comfortable, admits that she had not the ordinary human feelings for them, but nevertheless did her duty, and no one would have dreamed of the bitter sentiment which she so carefully concealed. Speaking of one such hospital scene a correspondent writes:

> Although the scene was a very sad one, yet its sorrow was abundantly relieved by the instances of warmhearted kindness and attention. We saw some jellies, custards, brandy, shirts, etc., which had been sent for the sick by some wholesouled ladies and gentlemen of this city. They have their reward in the grateful prayers of sick men, who are far away from home or friends. [54]

---

[54] *Corres. Wis. Volunteers*, vi, pp. 90, 91.

CONDITIONS AT HOME

Extravagance Rebuked

The hard times and depression which had characterized the middle period of the war gave place in 1864 to an era of reckless display and extravagance, combined with apparent callousness to the sufferings of others. Amusements were resumed on a gayer scale than formerly. Noble and serious-minded women were shocked, and protested against such frivolity and heedlessness. The Ladies' Union League of Madison prepared a pamphlet under the editorship of Mrs. J. W. Hoyt, Mrs. Edward Salomon, and Mrs. B. F. Hopkins, entitled "Retrenchment, the Duty of the Women of the North." They argued that while the national Government was facing such an extraordinary levy upon its funds, it was the duty of every member of the Federal family personally to assist in meeting the demand. The pamphlet argues:

We have before us the spectacle of our Government grappling with the most formidable rebellion that ever assaulted the nationality of any people * * * seeking to do all through its own resources, in order to avert the calamity of a large foreign indebtedness. No true American, man or woman, can contemplate this magnificence of preparation, this almost sublime spectacle of self-reliance, without being willing, without being anxious to add the savings of every judicious retrenchment to the national coffers.

That small class of persons who have an independence, or who are now accumulating fortunes, ought, furthermore, to do this as an example to those who have not such means, and who have yet the human nature to seek to imitate a style they cannot afford. It would be a good thought if every time an extravagant or superfluous article were about to be purchased, in reckoning the cost, the purchaser would add to this the value of that outlay some one else will make on this account.

WISCONSIN WOMEN IN THE WAR

The report further states that most of the members of the League depend upon business or professional support, and that many of the husbands and fathers belonging to that class are not making as much money as they were before the war:

With this large professional and business community rests the controlling ideas, as well as the largely controlling means of pushing successfully forward, or of untimely ending the war. It is possible, that the natural protectors of most of these families may, by unremitting energy and business devotion, maintain them in all the comfort and luxury of the past, notwithstanding the increased price of everything brought into household use. * * * But are we willing to see such efforts at such a time as this put forth to such an end—that of ease and appearance? How much more worthy our womanhood and this crisis, in every possible way to help lift the burden of the war from those on whom it mainly rests.

There is a still larger class of families, from whose circles a majority of those now in the field have gone. They are those, who, by the daily labor of both men and women, have been able to furnish themselves with the comforts and cheaper luxuries of life. Now, with the absence of the heads and older brothers and sons of these families, whose labor brought in the most of the little income, and the increased prices of goods and provisions, a state of real privation has come to exist. We cannot change all this. Our largest charities will not cover so large a ground. The only way in which we can meet our obligations to this class, is to help those in distress, and to those who are not, but who from the veriest of necessities are obliged to live cheaper, dress plainer, and work harder, set the example of ourselves doing without those extras that will on the one hand consume the money that ought to go in aid of the Government, and on the other, nourish the natural jealousy and discontent of the people. * * * The sympathy and confidence, that an entirely practicable retrenchment on our part would bring about

CONDITIONS AT HOME

between ourselves and this class of people, would react with a mighty force upon the rank and file of our armies.

A table retrenchment, that would touch the health and substantial comfort of any member of the household, would certainly be injudicious. The housekeeper holds the health and temper of her home pretty much in her own hands; and, without controversy, women maintain their empire over the opinions and actions of men largely through the fascinations of personal appearance.

What your committee would urge is, that we undertake to substitute good taste and a wholesome abundance in the place of parade and luxury, and that we make this the rule, not more for our families, than for social entertainments; and that, in our personal attire, we try the charm of a very decided plainness. * * *

Nothing but the direst necessity should induce us to cut off the supplies from which flow moral and religious education. The general charities and institutions of each community ought to be sustained, and it were well if this could be done even more liberally than before. [55]

The foregoing appeal shows better than any record, the spirit and ideals of the noblest of Wisconsin women. With such personalities at the head of Wisconsin charities and relief work, it is no wonder that the citizens of the State are proud of the part her women took in the Civil War.

---

[55] *Op. cit.*

Chapter V

Letters for the Front

Letters from home were the only connection which the soldiers had with their families except in a few rare cases, where women accompanied their soldier relatives to the front. If the home connection was once lost or broken the soldier was apt to be set adrift on a sea of loneliness and temptation. When it is taken into consideration that many of our volunteers were mere boys, the value of the home connection is even more apparent.

The soldier's craving for news from home was more positive than even his desire to end the cruel war. If he could have picked his place for winter-quarters at the front, he would have valued, as next to wood and water privileges, a station where home mail came regularly and promptly. [56]

A young volunteer thus describes the value of the home letters:

> We do not get letters enough to make us better men and better soldiers. We get the blues sometimes and feel like going to the dogs. The coffee is bad, the crackers worse, the bacon worst of all, and we are as hungry as wolves. Just then the mail boy brings in a letter, a good long one from you or from mother. * * * Immediately, all the weariness is gone; the fire has quit smoking, the musty, fusty crackers and bacon are

---

[56] Trumbull, *War Memoirs of a Chaplain* (New York, 1898), p. 148.

LETTERS FOR THE FRONT

better, and I am just the happiest fellow in the whole world. * * * One man, who was drunk yesterday, is crying tonight between the blankets, because he had a letter from his mother.

Another Wisconsin soldier looks at the matter from a psychological standpoint, and says:

Nothing gives more joy to a soldier, aside from meeting the enemy face to face, than a letter to break up the monotony of our peculiar style of life, and remind him of home and kindred spirits. * * * After a soldier has been out as long as we have, he only asks a chance to meet the enemy, get letters, and have enough hard crackers to eat. This to him is the sum total, the full perfection of a soldier's life. [57]

One soldier pleads with the readers of his letter to keep in as close communication with the soldier as possible, for he says:

A soldier after a little begins to lose his individuality and from being John Jones, Esquire, of Frogtown, he becomes only one of the Wisconsin Fifth or Indiana Nineteenth. He feels constantly among such a mass of men that he has lost his connection with the world, yea almost his personal identity, and that he is but part of a monster machine. A letter from home serves to dispel in great measure this feeling. [58]

Fortunately for the Wisconsin soldier, the Government made provision for regular and frequent distribution of the mail while the men were in the field or on the march. When possible it was brought to the point of distribution by boat; three whistles signified "mail." The ordinary procedure was for the regimental postmaster to go with his mail-bag to the city, in order to be present when the mail was dis-

---

[57] Livermore, p. 646.
[58] *Corres. Wis. Volunteers*, i, pp. 222-224.

tributed. Then he would hurry back to his tent, where he sorted the regimental mail which had been delivered to him. A writer speaks of the distribution as follows:

> It seemed as if the whole regiment gathered in sight of that postmaster's tent, as though longing eyes could quicken the work of busy fingers. There was but one thing thought of now. All hearts reached toward one center. Willing hands were ready to take the field-and-staff mail, when that was given out; but there was no need to carry it to regimental headquarters, for, from colonel to quartermaster, all were close by, waiting to receive what there was for them. The line-officers took their mail before it could reach their company street; and the men of each company followed their orderly sergeant, as he took their portion for distribution. Each face wore an anticipant look, and it would well repay the time spent in writing a letter, if the writers could only see the happy smiles or hear the happy exclamations of man after man, as their names were called. But when the mail is distributed, another sight greets you. Those who have not received anything, turn away to their quarters with sad, dejected looks, and now and then a murmur of "I'll get one next time." * * * If their friends could only see these desponding faces, they would not be so negligent in answering the poor "soger" boy's letter. [59]

It is evident that this writer did not think that the people at home were writing enough letters, but other facts prove that this conclusion was not correct. Women who lived during that time, speak of the great number of letters they wrote to the boys at the front; moreover, many letters did not reach their proper destination because incorrectly addressed. Even if letters were properly addressed they were often delayed in transmission. Moreover, the women were as anxious to hear from the soldiers as the

---

[59] Trumbull, pp. 133–139; *Corres. Wis. Volunteers*, i, p. 666.

IN FRONT OF A FIELD POSTMASTER'S TENT

From *The Photographic History of the Civil War;* copyright, 1911, by the Patriot Publishing Company. This contemporaneous photograph was taken at the quarters of the Chief Ambulance Officer, Ninth Army Corps, in front of Petersburg, Va., August, 1864. The tent is in a small grove of pine trees, through which the sun is streaming with torrid heat

LETTERS FOR THE FRONT

latter were to hear from home, and this incentive in itself was enough to keep up an active exchange.

Letters for Strangers

It is well known that Wisconsin women wrote not only to their own friends and relatives, but also to men whom they had never seen. "We girls felt it a patriotic duty not to leave any of the boys unsolaced by cheery and newsy letters," states one of the women. Often into comfort bags would be slipped a note that evoked a reply. One Wisconsin girl had a long and pleasant correspondence of this kind, until the young man revealed himself and proposed marriage; then she stopped. After the war one of our most honored matrons, then only a maiden in her teens, found a handsome young soldier at the door ready to complete the acquaintance begun in this way, and Beloit was the scene of a new home. [60]

Sometimes young girls wrote letters to men who received none, having heard of their disappointment from friends in the army. Occasionally, thoughtful women wrote a number of unaddressed letters and sent them to some friend among the troops with instructions to distribute them where they were most needed.

The case of a woman in a little Northern town is typical of the amount of letter-writing done during the war period. Her husband had gone to the front, leaving her with a four weeks old baby, yet she kept on writing letters to all her relatives, including not only her husband, but three brothers-in-law, and three cousins. Her communications went to three hospitals.

---
[60] Ms. letter from Miss Simmons.

WISCONSIN WOMEN IN THE WAR

Although the majority of the soldiers and their families corresponded in this way, there were a few cases where neither the soldier nor his home relatives could read and write, and there would have been no connection between them and their families at all had it not been for unselfish Wisconsin women, who wrote their letters for them. The writers usually made such letters as realistic as possible and told the details concerning the soldier's family and home, how the children were behaving, what diseases they had, how the crops looked, etc. The man who received such a letter would get a friend to read it for him and in course of time some one would reply at his dictation; thus communication was kept up between the home and the field.

Letters from the Field

If letters from home were appreciated in the army, those from the army were fully as much appreciated at home. Such letters were not regarded as private property; they were sent around from one interested person to another until at last they were returned to their respective owners. The soldiers realized this, and consequently they mentioned in their letters this person or that one who lived in the neighborhood, and to whom the letters should be sent. Occasionally they enclosed battle-clippings and lists of the killed and wounded.

The men, however, often received more army news than they gave, for the people at home knew from the newspapers more about the army in general than the soldier in one small division could. The women in their letters enclosed pictures of battlefields and clippings of all kinds which they had collected; and often they used paper and

LETTERS FOR THE FRONT

envelopes decorated with patriotic emblems in order to show their interest in martial affairs.

Difficulties of Letter Writing

If it was difficult for the women to write letters it was even more so for the soldier to answer them. In many cases the poor fellows had no stamps, and as one says, "If friends do not receive replies to their letters as quickly as they wish, they will readily understand the reason,"[61] which was, of course, an invitation for the person receiving the letter to enclose a postage stamp when replying.

Moreover, the soldiers had no convenient places for writing. They described vividly the attitudes they were forced to adopt. Some sat on logs and wrote by the light of candles, others lay flat on their stomachs, still others used their knapsacks for tables. But whatever the attitude the writing was kept up throughout the war.

The following quotation shows the kind of letters soldiers most appreciated:

> A soldier far away from home does not care to hear of all the little troubles his friends are undergoing, for he cannot help them, and he has enough on his mind without having his letters filled with gloom; but if his friends would only show the bright side of the picture it would encourage him to make himself altogether different from what he is.[62]

The moral effect of letters from home was greater than we realize; just as the value of personal influence is hard to measure, so was the effect which was produced by these home letters. Many of the soldiers were kept to their duty

---

[61] *Corres. Wis. Volunteers,* I, p. 66.
[62] *Id.,* v, p. 170.

WISCONSIN WOMEN IN THE WAR

by such letters, and many were kept from vice of all sorts by a word of advice or warning from the faraway wife or mother. It is good to look back and to remember what a close connection was preserved with the home by the exchange of letters, and to know that Wisconsin women did their full duty in this respect.

Chapter VI

Women with the Regiments

Wisconsin soldiers, on leaving their home towns, usually went into camp at some place within the State for some weeks or months before being sent to the front. Frequently their wives accompanied them thither, or came on later in order to say a last goodbye. Occasionally the wives of officers accompanied their husbands even farther. When the Sixth Regiment left for the front, eight or ten of the officers' wives accompanied them; all but one returned, however, after having reached Harrisburg. A soldier in the Sixth writes: "All these ladies have been very pleasant companions, but I think they had better have stayed at home." Another vounteer writes in the same strain about women in the army: "This advice is based upon observation. There are no provisions made for them, and they are regarded as outsiders by the authorities, and their friends have no time to provide for them."[63]

Fortunately for the women, other views were held by many. One of the soldiers who took up cudgels in their defense, argues in the following manner: "As far as impropriety is concerned, a few women are as well off or better off, among a thousand men, than they would be with a single man." He asserts that this is true, because men

---

[63] *Id.*, i, pp. 217, 238.

WISCONSIN WOMEN IN THE WAR

demand from each other exact conduct toward the women entrusted to their care, and thus women are better protected in the army than in their homes. The writer also maintains that a woman's presence, for the moral effect, is needed in camp just as much as at home. "A rough, almost tameless man, while in the presence of women, becomes watchful over every word passing his lips; he minds his walk, would not appear filthy, desires more intelligence, and has more pride when women are about than if all were men."[64]

Daughters of the Regiment

Two Wisconsin regiments were accompanied to the field by young women who played the difficult part of daughters of the regiment. The first of these was the Fifth, with whom went Miss Eliza, daughter of William Wilson of Menomonie, Dunn County, former member of the State Senate, and possessed of considerable wealth. Miss Wilson had her own tent and servant, and furnished with necessary food and clothing went out with the regiment on her philanthropic mission. She was to pay all of her own expenses, and her duties were to head the regiment when on parade, and to assuage the thirst of the wounded and dying on the battlefield, where it was hoped that she would be a real guardian angel of the regiment. Miss Wilson was well chaperoned, for several of her relatives were in the regiment, besides a number of men lately in the employ of her father. A description of her appearance is given in the following words:

Eliza is decidedly smart and intelligent, of medium size, amiable, twenty, and pretty. She dresses in clothes of such

[64] *Ibid*, p. 217.

WITH THE REGIMENTS

pattern as the military (not millinery) board have ordered for nurses in the army, which is the Turkish costume, as near as I can judge—the same which sensible ladies favored a few years since as a national style. The color is bright brown; no crinoline; dress reaches half way between the knee and ankle; upper sleeve loose, gathered at the wrist; pantalettes same color, wide but gathered tight around the ankle; black hat with plumes or feathers of same color; feet dressed in morocco boots. This vivandière dress is no hindrance to rapid movements; fast walking is a graceful exercise, while the slow inevitable strut of crinoline appears awkward to the lady dressed in army costume. [65]

From later letters it is evident that Eliza was useful as well as ornamental, for she took care of sick soldiers and "by her continued kind attentions to and care for them has merited and is receiving the blessings of those who were ready to perish in the absence of her kindness."

Another soldier, who wrote two months later, says:

The boys have no sweethearts to see, and therefore white shirts, standing collars, hair-oil, bosom-pins and tight boots have disappeared completely. We have not seen a woman for a fortnight with the exception of the Daughter of the Regiment, who is with us in storm and sunshine. It would do you good to see her trudging along, with or after the regiment, her dark brown frock buttoned tightly around her waist, her what-you-call-ems tucked into her well fitting gaiters, her hat and feather set jauntily on one side, her step firm and assured, for she knows that every arm in our ranks would protect her. Never pouting or passionate, with a kind word for every one, and every one a kind word for her. She came with one of the companies and remains with the regiment. Were it not for her, when a woman would appear, we would be running after her, as children do after an organ and a monkey. [66]

---
[65] *Ibid*, p. 216.
[66] *Ibid*, pp. 218, 225.

WISCONSIN WOMEN IN THE WAR

It appears that Eliza did not tire of doing good, for she is still mentioned in January, 1862, as being with the regiment, only she had been quite ill, "which elicited much sympathy" from her comrades. [67]

The other daughter of the regiment of whom we have an account was Hannah Ewbank, a school-mistress of Marquette, who joined the Seventh Regiment. A description of her is given in the following words:

> In the matter of teaching the young idea how to shoot, Miss Ewbank bore an enviable reputation; but deeming her sphere limited, she has joined the Grand Army, where she may encourage the elder ideas to shoot in a manner peculiarly desirable, and which recommends itself to every patriotic mind. Her uniform is very neat, consisting of a Zouave jacket of blue merino, trimmed with military buttons and gold lace; a skirt of scarlet merino, trimmed with blue and gold lace; pants and vest of white Marseilles; balmoral boots; hat of blue velvet trimmed with white and gold lace, with yellow plumes, and white kid gloves. A more jaunty or bewitching little Daughter of the Regiment never handled the canteen, and it is no wonder that the multiplex father jealously watches her, and has sworn sacredly to defend her. [68]

In Masculine Garb

It would be interesting to know how many Wisconsin women, disguised as men, served in the ranks, but the question will probably never be answered, except in circulating rumors, connected with this or that woman who wore masculine attire. Two well authenticated cases are known.

---

[67] *Id.*, iii, p. 277.

[68] Undated newspaper clipping, loaned to author by Mrs. Martha Showalter, Lancaster.

WITH THE REGIMENTS

In the town of Lake Mills lived a devoted sister and brother, Sarah and Mason Collins. When the war broke out, Mason made up his mind to enlist, and his courageous sister decided to do the same. She was a robust girl with the bloom of roses upon her cheeks, and could easily have borne the hardships incident to a soldier's life. Won over by her persistence, her brother Mason aided and abetted the deception; her tresses were cut short, she put on man's apparel, and endeavored to accustom herself to her strange garb. She accompanied her brother to the rendezvous of the company, and notwithstanding her soldier-like appearance and air of masculinity, her sex was detected—it is stated, by her unmasculine manner of putting on her shoes and stockings. So poor Sarah, with tears in her eyes, disappointed at the failure of her efforts to become a soldier, was obliged to return to her home, while her brother left for the front without her.[69]

The other case recorded is that of Belle Peterson, a young country girl, who lived near Ellenboro. A soldier who saw her at that time, says that she was "just an ordinary girl, neither good nor bad looking." But she was adventurous, and one day surprised her father by telling him that she was going away from home for some time. Her family learned later that she had enlisted in a Wisconsin regiment. The date of her enlistment is not certain, but it was probably late in 1862; she served in the army for some time, possibly as a spy or a scout. Those who saw her in her uniform, say that she made a fair-looking soldier, and that no one would have suspected that she was a woman.[70]

---

[69] Ms. loaned by E. W. Keyes (Madison, 1910).
[70] Ms. letter of L. D. Culver (Ellenboro, Wis., May, 1910).

WISCONSIN WOMEN IN THE WAR

Officers' Wives

Letters from Wisconsin soldiers prove that the Seventh, Eighth, and Eleventh regiments were accompanied by Wisconsin women. On Thanksgiving Day, 1862, the Eleventh Regiment had a dinner, given by the Colonel's wife for the officers and their wives. Concerning it a soldier writes, "Eating turkey on china plates, we could hardly realize we were in camp."[71] On New Year's Day, 1862, the Seventh Regiment "was graced by the presence of several ladies. It was quite a novelty to all and hugely enjoyed; the ladies joining in the repartees of wit which passed from one end of the table to the other."[72] In April, 1862, a member of the Third Wisconsin Cavalry writes from St. Louis: "Several of the tents are graced by the wives and ladies of the officers, which adds much to the social caste of our regiment, and is an agreeable phase of the patriotic sympathy which the fair daughters of our Union are pleased to bestow upon our cause and upon the defenders."[73]

Interesting interviews occasionally took place between these Northern women and the Southerners in their neighborhood. For the most part the Northerners were not so bitter as their Southern sisters. On one occasion, however, they had a chance to speak their minds to the women champions of "Secessia." Two officers' wives were visiting a Wisconsin regiment which was stationed at Bear Creek, Mississippi. They called frequently on the ladies

---

[71] *Corres. Wis. Volunteers*, ii, p. 43.
[72] *Id.*, iii, p. 279.
[73] *Id.*, vii, p. 209.

residing in the neighborhood; in one or two instances a collision was with difficulty averted. The narrator remarks: "I tell you, the women of the North are beginning to feel combative. They won't stand secesh talk. But we have quieted them down now, pretty well. We made them believe that it was unconstitutional for the women to quarrel and fight, but it would not require very heavy reinforcements from the North to get the women started on a big raid." [74]

A good story is told of the wife of a Wisconsin congressman, who in 1861 was visiting at Arlington Heights. She was seated in a carriage, when the Sixth Wisconsin passed, whereupon she inquired the name of the regiment. It was usually called the "Baby Sixth," a nickname for "King's pet babies;" so a lieutenant standing by answered, "The Baby Sixth, Ma'am." The lady, not understanding the joke, which was more complimentary than otherwise, indignantly replied, "Sir! I am from Wisconsin, and allow me to inform you, that we send no infants to war from there." [75]

While Mrs. Salomon, the Governor's wife, was traveling in the South, she visited the hospitals in St. Louis in order to find out how the Wisconsin soldiers were being treated; later she went to Rolla, Missouri, where an enthusiastic reception was given her. She describes it as follows:

> The reception, which we received by our brave officers and men, surpassed any expectations I could have formed. The camps were decorated with green boughs and trees, a magnificent dining hall was improvised—made of green branches

---

[74] *Id.*, i, p. 265.
[75] *Ibid*, p. 265.

WISCONSIN WOMEN IN THE WAR

entirely, and having within its green folds one of the finest festive boards I ever sat down at. All was gladness, animation, health, and life. Every one seemed rejoiced to see us, and I can assure you, that the fatigues of the journey were quickly forgotten and amply repaid by the hearty welcome and smiling faces around us. The dining hall was one hundred and twenty feet long. The guests, including nearly thirty ladies, numbered about one hundred and fifty. * * * The day was finished with a ball, given by our officers in an unfinished school house. [76]

Mrs. Lyon's Services

Although the women of the North were much appreciated in the army on social occasions, they were in the South for far more important tasks—as home-makers, nurses, and mothers to whole regiments. In these duties they showed their seriousness of purpose. Mrs. W. P. Lyon was one of these women. Her husband was Colonel first of the Eighth, later of the Thirteenth Regiment. Although she was only a young woman at this time, the men of the regiment who did not call her "mother" spoke of her as the regiment's angel, for she spent her days in visiting and cheering the sick in hospitals, in preparing dainties to tempt their appetites, and in writing letters to their dear ones at home. There was probably not a member of the regiment who would not have risked his life to shield his good friend from danger. The following anecdote, recorded in a Wisconsin newspaper, shows why the soldiers almost worshipped Mrs. Lyon:

> One night, she saw a soldier carrying a rail as a punishment. "How much longer must you carry that heavy thing?"
> "Until morning, Madam."

---

[76] *Id.*, ix, p. 317.

WITH THE REGIMENTS

"When did you eat last?"

"This morning, and can't eat again until tomorrow." The little woman returned to the Colonel's tent and begged him to pardon the poor fellow, and let him get something to eat.

"I can't do that, my dear, but this I will do. You get up a good supper for him, and I will carry his rail while he eats," which was accordingly done, to the great satisfaction of Mrs. Lyon and the soldier. [77]

Deaths of Women in the Army

Several of the Wisconsin women who went South died there, far from their homes. The soldiers, writing about these deaths, seemed to feel in each case, that the woman's life was the price of her devotion to her husband. Referring to the death of a young sergeant's wife, one correspondent says: "At the time of her death, they had only been married about five months, and the heroic young wife had left all the luxuries of a Wisconsin fireside to share the toils and privations of a camp life with her husband in Virginia." [78] Another soldier writes:

The wife of Sergeant Williams of Company I, Seventh Regiment, died in camp of typhoid fever. * * * She was sick but eight days. The camp of the soldier is no place for a woman, either to live or die in. Patriotism and love for her kindred may induce a woman to surrender the comforts and quiet of home for the privations and hardships of the camp; but it is no place for her, and in nine cases out of ten, she will be more an inconvenience than an advantage, either as a nurse or a laundress. [79]

---

[77] Janesville *Gazette*, April 18, 1910.
[78] *Corres. Wis. Volunteers*, iii, p. 247.
[79] *Id.*, ii, p. 1.

Chapter VII

Hospitals and Nurses

The provision made by the Government for the comfort and health of the soldiers was anything but satisfactory at the outbreak of the war. The country was unprepared for the emergencies of warfare; so much unnecessary misery and suffering ensued, especially during the first two years of the war.

The volunteers started off in cheerful spirits, with sound bodies, ready to endure all necessary inconveniences for the sake of their country. Their patriotism was, however, severely tried at the start, for "they were crowded into cars like beasts, with empty haversacks." Only occasionally were they given food and coffee as they passed through the various towns "en route." Yet worse was the reception they met when they reached their destination. They had often to stand for hours in the broiling sunshine or in the drenching rain, while quartermasters and commissaries learned their duties. The result was, that the volunteers reached camp utterly disgusted with their surroundings and rations; while many fell easy prey to disease.[80]

Early Hospitals

The early hospital arrangements were almost as bad as the facilities for transportation; the buildings were not

---

[80] Livermore, p. 123.

HOSPITALS AND NURSES

suitable, and there was an alarming dearth of supplies in every department. A letter from a Wisconsin volunteer, written in November, 1861, confirms these reports:

As yet we have done little fighting, but have lost a large number of men. They are dying daily in the camps and hospitals, from pneumonia, dysentery, and camp diseases, caused by severe colds, exposure, and lack of proper food when ill. * * * For two days and nights there was a very severe storm, to which we were exposed all the time, wearing shoddy uniforms and protected only by shoddy blankets, and the result was a frightful sickness.

Our hospitals are so bad that the men fight against being sent to them. * * * I really believe, they are more comfortable and better cared for in camp with their comrades, than in hospitals. The food is the same in both places, and the medical treatment the same, if there is any. In the hospital the sick men lie on rotten straw; in the camp we provide clean hemlock or pine boughs, with the stems cut out, or husks when we can jerk them from a secesh cornfield.

We need beds and bedding, hospital clothing and sick diet, proper medicines, surgical instruments, and good nurses—and then a decent building or a good hospital tent for the accommodation of the sick. I suppose we shall have them, when the Government can get around to it, and in the meantime we try to be patient. [81]

Another soldier writes in December, 1862, "One could not expect all members of a great army to enjoy all the comforts of home, but the gross neglect with which sick men are treated is enough to horrify a person of common sensibilities."[82]

---

[81] *Ibid*, pp. 126, 127.
[82] *Corres. Wis. Volunteers*, iii, p. 147.

WISCONSIN WOMEN IN THE WAR

Women as Nurses

Not only were hospitals in need of improvement, but the nursing staff at first was inadequate to the demand. When this became known, numbers of women, many without knowledge, experience, or known fitness for the vocation, offered themselves for service. Fortunately there was one woman whose experience and temperament fitted her to organize and direct the work of nurses in the United States. Dorothea Dix was early appointed superintendent of women nurses by the Secretary of War; her duties being "to select and appoint women as nurses and to assign them to the general or permanent military hospitals." Without her sanction and approval, no woman could enter such hospitals as a nurse, except in cases of emergency.[83]

In October, 1863, additional regulations were adopted, placing more authority in the hands of Miss Dix and limiting to thirty the number of beds one nurse could be placed in charge of.

Opposed by Surgeons

When women first offered their services to the Government as nurses, they had much to contend with, for few hospital surgeons were in favor of their employment. After the Government had decided to utilize them, the surgeons were unable to close the hospitals against them, but they could and did make their lives almost unbearable; it seems that their behavior was based on the cool calculation as to

---

[83] Tarbell, "American Women," in *American Magazine*, lxix, pp. 802, 806; *Rebellion Records*, Serial 124, p. 943.

HOSPITALS AND NURSES

how much ill-mannered opposition would be requisite to break up the system. One of the nurses said:

> Some of the bravest women I have ever known, were among this first company of army nurses. They saw at once the position of affairs, the attitude assumed by the surgeons, and the wall against which they were expected to break and scatter; and they set themselves to work to undermine the whole thing. None of them were strong minded. Some of them were women of the truest refinement and culture; and day after day they quietly and patiently worked, doing by orders of the surgeons, things which not one of those gentlemen would have dared ask of a woman, whose male relative stood able and ready to defend her and report him. I have seen small white hands scrubbing floors, washing windows, and performing all menial offices. I have known women, delicately cared for at home, half fed in hospitals, hard worked day and night and given, when sleep must be had, a wretched closet, just large enough for a camp bed to stand in. [84]

Surgeons often arranged all the details of their work with the avowed intention of driving out the women. Thus did "professional etiquette put its cold paw on private benevolence." [85] The nurses endured such treatment because they were pioneers, and had the satisfaction of seeing the sick and dying men comforted in their weary and final hours. At last surgeons began to see that the lives saved by these women reflected credit upon themselves, and that their resistance to their employment was unmanly.

---

[84] Georgeanna W. Bacon and Eliza W. Howland, *Letters of a Family during the War for the Union* (privately printed, 1899), i, pp. 142, 143.

[85] *Ibid*, p. 145.

WISCONSIN WOMEN IN THE WAR

Wisconsin Nurses

Among Wisconsin nurses was a Miss Hadley, who began her work after the battle of Fort Donelson, and continued it on a floating hospital at Pittsburg Landing. In April, 1862, while on the boat, she wrote:

I was awakened on the Sabbath morning by the roar of cannon and musketry, and in a few moments the operations of my toilet were accelerated double-quick by the groans of the wounded. The log-cabin was speedily filled with bleeding, suffering humanity, and Mrs. Turner and myself soon realized, though not for the first time, that women have a more serious mission than haranguing public assemblies, and with all their wrongs a few rights perhaps. It was: "Oh! Mrs. T., Oh! Miss H. How glad we are you are here"—and as one and another bloodstained countenance brightened at our approach, we thanked heaven we *were* here. So through the dreadful days we soothed and encouraged, hoped and prayed, for the enemy's shells burst within twenty yards of our boat. I was as calm as at this moment, and never doubted we should whip them at last. I fear I horrify you, but I do not think I have grown hard hearted, though I can now write of scenes from which I should once have run with closed eyes. [86]

Another vivid description of the horrors on board a hospital ship was written in 1862, by W. E. Wording of Racine, member of the Wisconsin Sanitary Commission, whose wife was unceasing in her devotion to the sick. "No pen or brush or human tongue can paint the loathsome horrors, now visible on our boat. In spite of all that can be done by physicians and their attendants, the dying and the dead, the delirious and the convalescing, all mingled together, the groans, the gasping sufferers, and the intol-

---

[86] *Corres. Wis. Volunteers*, v, p. 233.

HOSPITALS AND NURSES

erable stench, all combine to make up a picture of human woe, that no human art can realize, no human imagination conceive."[87]

Among the few Wisconsin nurses now living, is Mrs. Susannah Van Valkenburg of Oshkosh; she is a type of the independent nurse, who did such effective work in Southern hospitals. In 1863 she went with her husband to Alexandria, Virginia, where she remained for seven months. Being a woman of warm impulses and strong sympathies, and withal physically and temperamentally fitted for the task, she accomplished much during her short stay at the front. Her first experience was at the Wolf Street hospital, where the pitiful scenes affected her very much at first, but she wiped away her tears and walked over to a cot where a boy lay, seemingly unconscious. Touching his forehead she said: "Do you know that I have come all the way from Wisconsin to care for sick and wounded soldiers like yourself? Will you not look up and speak to me? I will try to fill a mother's or a sister's place, if you will allow me to."

He looked up, saying slowly as if dazed, "Will you?" "Try me and see. Your nurse tells me, that you have not tasted food for three days. Think of what you would have asked your mother or sister for, and, if possible, I will get it for you." With an indescribable look of joy on his face the boy answered, "Can you make biscuits, like my mother used to make?" She assured him that she could, if the surgeon consented. That official looked at her in amazement, but answered: "Give him what he wants; he cannot live," whereupon the biscuits were made. On

---
[87] *Ibid*. p. 270.

the nurse's way back to the hospital, she passed one of Alexandria's beautiful residences; to its owner she applied for a jar of jelly. "Sparkling eyes and an eager smile" wreathed the suffering face, as she appeared with the wished-for dainties; the memory of the satisfaction she had afforded the sick boy never left her. From that very day the boy began to improve, and as he grew stronger, he used to creep to the window to watch for the pleasant-faced woman, as she was called by the inmates of the hospital.[88]

After Mrs. Van Valkenburg had been at Wolf Street hospital a short time, the superintendent of the United States Christian Commission learned of her gratuitous labors; he offered to place the supplies in the custody of that organization at her disposal; this privilege she availed herself of very often. In January, 1864, she was transferred to King Street hospital, where she remained until illness forced her to give up her work. At the latter hospital she was allowed to enter the wards at all hours of the day and night; a privilege she often made use of, for in May, 1864, a number of wounded soldiers were brought in, who sadly needed her constant care. At one time she solicited from Battery A a sum of money, which she expended in buying lemons and sugar, with which she made lemonade in two large camp-kettles. Nearly every hospital in Alexandria received its share, and the gratitude of the soldiers for the cooling drink was touching. Through the generosity of a wealthy woman who had seen her trudging back and forth to the hospital, laden with supplies, she was enabled to

---

[88] Grand Army Publishing Company, *Soldiers' and Citizens' Album of Biographical Record, Wisconsin* (Chicago, 1888), i, p. 647.

HOSPITALS AND NURSES

serve the boys with soup; on the days designated Mrs. Van Valkenburg and four boys in blue who helped her, received two large camp-boilers of soup for the sick soldiers.

But the activities of this helpful woman were not confined to hospitals alone; she made the small cottage her husband had built in Battery B, a social center for the soldier boys, who ran in and out as though it was their home, and she their mother. So comfortable was the little cottage, that the captain of the Commission brought a Massachusetts officer to see "what a home a Wisconsin woman could make in a soldier's camp." Yet it was only a room twelve feet square and built of the plainest materials. [89] At entertainments and in the various churches she took an active part in the singing. She used also to write letters for the soldiers, conveying the last message of the dying, or inquiring if the keepsakes of the dead soldier had reached their proper destination; if they had been kept back for any reason, Mrs. Van Valkenburg made it her duty to report the matter, and force the guilty person to give up the articles.

As a type of strong, sane womanhood, and of vigorous, unselfish service, Mrs. Van Valkenburg should be regarded as one of the first in the list of Wisconsin women of the Civil War period.

Occasionally a Wisconsin woman served as hospital matron; a news item from Camp Randall states that the wife of the orderly to the colonel of the Eighth Regiment was to go with her husband in that capacity. [90]

July 1, 1864, the wages of hospital matrons were increased

---
[89] *Ibid*, p. 647.
[90] *Corres. Wis. Volunteers*, ii, p. 6.

[115]

WISCONSIN WOMEN IN THE WAR

to ten dollars a month and rations.[91] When the responsibility and difficulty of such a position is considered, the compensation seems almost ridiculously inadequate.

Sanitary Agents

Another phase of women's work in the hospitals was the distribution of sanitary supplies. For this purpose several Wisconsin women then living in Washington were appointed. The experience of one of these agents in October, 1862, throws much light upon hospital conditions. The camp which she visited, contained 16,000 men. These merely existed under the terrible conditions they were subjected to; 1,000 of these soldiers had no shirts, many were ill with typhoid fever, and were lying in the sand and dirt with no pillows under their heads. Hundreds of the "poor filthy fellows" followed her, which made it necessary to have a guard to clear the way. In relating her experiences of those dreadful days, she says:

> I went to the sanitary room and took some three hundred shirts, two hundred pillows, crackers, fruit, condensed milk, blankets, etc. One poor man from Wisconsin, the most like a living skeleton I ever saw, to whom I gave a blanket, being a little delirious, kept repeating to himself and to others, "Have not got to shiver tonight," over and over again. I came home determined to do something for them and went to Mr. and Mrs. L., to the surgeon-general, and to the medical purveyor; and yesterday I visited most of the committees to get all I could, and today I go out with a number of distributors. I gathered enough to take four wagons, besides half a boat-load, and sixteen persons for distributors when there. I have just been out with my ambulance and bought seven barrels of onions, ten of pota-

---

[91] *Rebellion Records*, Serial 125, p. 512.

HOSPITALS AND NURSES

toes, twelve hundred shirts, one thousand sheets, two hundred drawers, four hundred pants, six barrels of dried fruit, twelve pairs of crutches, five hundred pillows and cases, seventy quilts, one hundred pounds of condensed beef, sixty cans of beef soup, and eighty cushions for wounded limbs, etc. But this among so many is but very little. * * *

Oh! such scenes, such tears, such expressions of gratitude— it was enough to break my heart. * * * Multitudes thronged around, begging for things. I told them I would give them all something if they would keep off. But, O, such pleading and begging, "Please, madam, give me a shirt, I have not had one in two months." "Please give me a pair of socks or shoes, I have not had any these four months, and you can see how sore and swollen my feet are." They stood four deep, two lines each side of me full four rods long, just as close as possible. * * * I first ascertained by the aid of the officer of the day, who had no shirts and gave to them first and then to others, as discreetly as I could. We then opened the onions, some of them, and so many begged and pleaded for one raw, we could find no place to stop till two half barrels were given out. * * * But understand that after all that we gave * * * only the sickest and a few others were supplied. The mass are without beds, without even straw to lie on, nor even grass, the ground being trampled on by so great a crowd, eighteen thousand. * * * The second one I spoke to in the hospital was from Wisconsin, and O, how his eye brightened, as I said "These things came from your own home." [92]

Thus it may be seen, that Wisconsin women did their full share of work in the South, as nurses, matrons, and sanitary agents. It was also largely due to their efforts and to those of other Northern women, that the hospitals were made places of comfort and cheer, instead of being unclean, unsanitary holes, unfit for human beings to occupy.

[92] *Corres. Wis. Volunteers*, ii, p. 319.

Chapter VIII

Mrs. Cordelia A. P. Harvey

Among the women whom the Civil War brought to the front as leaders, such as Louisa Lee Schuyler, Dorothea Dix, and Anna Dickinson, Mrs. Cordelia A. Perrine Harvey from Wisconsin, deserves a place. In some respects she was a national figure, one of the great army-nurses whose work was not limited by state lines.

Early Life

The early life of this remarkable woman did not differ from that of other Wisconsin women of her day, who spent their lives in small towns, busy with the daily routine. She lived for many years in Kenosha, where her father's family, the Perrines, were prominent in the decade of the forties. There she taught school, and there she was married to a school-teacher, Louis P. Harvey. In 1845, the young couple moved to Clinton Junction where Mr. Harvey kept a country store. Thence they removed their home to Shopiere in Rock County, where they remained until 1859, when Mr. Harvey's election as Secretary of State made his presence in Madison necessary. Mr. Harvey was a person of strong personality and political sagacity, and in 1861 the people of Wisconsin elected him Governor. From the day of the firing on Fort Sumter both he and his wife showed a deep interest in the Civil War. A company of

MRS. HARVEY

volunteers were named for the Governor, the "Harvey Zouaves;" to each of its members Mrs. Harvey presented a Bible and a Testament; with additional remembrances for the officers.

In the busy days which followed the first call for troops, Mrs. Harvey entered with enthusiasm into work for the soldiers and their families. She was enabled to give her time, because she and her husband were boarding and she was not cumbered with household duties.

Governor Harvey's Death

Governor Harvey went to the South in the spring of 1862 in order to learn whether the sick and wounded Wisconsin men were well cared for. He stopped at Cairo, Mound City, and Paducah, in each case making visits to hospitals, where the sick of Wisconsin regiments were located. The Governor's deep sympathy is shown by the following comment in one of the reports from the front:

It would have moved a heart of stone to witness the interviews between the Governor and our wounded heroes. There was something more than formality about these visits, and the men knew it by sure instinct. [93]

At Pittsburg Landing the same was even more evident:

The news of the Governor's arrival spread as if by magic, and at every house those who could stand clustered around him, and those who had not raised their heads for days, sat up, their faces aglow with gratitude for the kind looks, and words and acts, which showed the Governor's tender care of them. At times these scenes were so affecting, that even the Governor's self-control failed him, and he could not trust himself to talk.

---

[93] *Id.*, v, pp. 236, 237.

WISCONSIN WOMEN IN THE WAR

When he had done everything in his power for the Wisconsin men, he went to Savannah, seven miles away, his heart filled with well-earned satisfaction as a result of his labors. From there he wrote to his wife: "Yesterday was *the* day of my life. Thank God for the impulse, that brought me here. I am well, and have done more good by coming, than I can well tell you." [94]

At Savannah, Tennessee, as he was about to pass from one boat to another, his foot slipped, and he fell into the water and was drowned, before help could be secured.

While this tragic event was taking place, his wife, totally unconscious of the shocking incident, was busily engaged in collecting money for the relief of soldiers' families. When the dispatch containing the distressing news was received by Adjutant-General Gaylord, Mrs. Harvey was at the capitol, securing subscriptions in order to aid a destitute family in the city. An attempt was made to get her to her boarding house, before the contents of the dispatch were made known, but Mrs. Harvey understood at once, by the faces of the men present, that some bad news had been received. Her friends tried to accompany her home, and Mr. Gaylord told her that a rumor had been received, which gave him some anxiety in regard to the Governor. While they were attempting to conceal the full extent of the calamity, she stopped and said, "Tell me if he is dead!" Mr. Gaylord evaded a direct reply, but she read the fatal news in the expression of his face and fainted. She was taken home, where for a short time her grief unsettled her mind. [95]

[94] Tuttle, p. 700.
[95] *Corres. Wis. Volunteers*, v, pp. 237, 238.

MRS. HARVEY

She was not a woman to spend her life in mourning, however, and when the intensity of her grief had somewhat lessened, she began to ask herself what her duties in life were to be. While in this state of mind, she came to realize the whole import of her husband's character, of which his last letter to her was but an index. This feeling took such a strong possession of her, that a settled conviction possessed her that her duty in life was to finish the work which he had left undone.[96] With a woman of her temperament, to will was to act. She soon therefore began to inquire where and how she could be most helpful to Wisconsin soldiers.

An extract from a letter of Judge Howe, dated August 27, 1862, shows what plans her friends made for her:[97]

Mrs. Harvey is visiting us. You can imagine something how she suffers from the loss of her husband. Her friends desire that she should find employment with which to occupy her mind. But what employment can a woman find? She is urged to try a school for young ladies, but she fears the derangement of the times will forbid success, and so do I. She has thought of a hospital, but you know General Hammond is taking them under his own care exclusively, and her strength will not warrant her in contracting for day labor.

This morning I suggested to her the idea of being appointed allotment commissioner in place of Mr. Holton. It pleases her. It is a kind of missionary labor, to which she is fully equal, and in which she will be, I am confident, very successful. I know no one more energetic than she is in whatever interests her. You know how deeply she has interested herself in the welfare of the army. She could plead the cause of a soldier's family to the soldier himself, I think, with great effect.

---

[96] Tuttle, p. 700.

[97] Ms. letter of Judge Howe to Judge Doolittle (Green Bay, Aug. 27, 1862).

WISCONSIN WOMEN IN THE WAR

The duties of an allotment commissioner were to visit the different companies in order to ascertain what proportion of the soldier's wages he would send home in monthly or other installments. This money was to be placed at the disposal of the families of the volunteers. Considering the soldier's temptation, this system was a very useful one; it apportioned part of his pay by his own act, in order to support his family. [98]

Sanitary Agent

This was not, however, to be her work. September 10, 1862, Governor Salomon appointed her sanitary agent at St. Louis, and for the succeeding four years she rendered acceptable service in the Southland for Wisconsin soldiers. [99]

It will be easier to understand the secret of her success in the South, if we realize what manner of woman she was. From all accounts she was not beautiful, although possessed of a strong, magnetic personality, and delightfully frank, yet charming manners. Her tact was unusual, therefore she succeeded in accomplishing things in which other people failed. United with this tact was an indomitable will and an untiring persistence. With such characteristics it might be imagined that she lacked in tenderness and sympathy. Such was not the case, however; her motherly heart and sympathetic nature caused the men to call her the "Wisconsin Angel." United to these qualities of character and temperament was her experience in social affairs; she knew how to approach those

---
[98] *Corres. Wis. Volunteers*, v, p. 247.
[99] Quiner, p. 126.

MRS. HARVEY

in high official positions as well as the humblest private. Withal, she had a fine sense of humor, a fund of homely common sense, and a deep religious feeling, which expressed itself in deeds rather than in words. She was always modest and often said that every patriotic woman in Wisconsin deserved as much praise as she. In short, she was an extremely human, lovable person, of the highest type of womanhood, unselfish, unconsciously great, and Wisconsin can forever be proud of having the honor to claim her as its daughter.

Early in the fall of 1862, Mrs. Harvey went to St. Louis as sanitary agent. Timidly and carefully she felt her way, at first seeking to comprehend the necessities of the situation, for other intelligent and worthy women had failed when attempting what she was assigned to undertake.[1] She found the medical department poorly organized, and hampered by many incompetent surgeons. Although she realized the delicacy of the situation she was firm in her opinion that conditions must be radically changed, even if the sacred red-tape of government rules had to be cut. She began by visiting hospitals, in order that she might find out where improvements were most needed. She stayed for several weary weeks at St. Louis, where she visited the hospitals at Benton Barracks and Fifth Street; these were crowded with men from the camps and battlefields of Missouri and Tennessee.

At Cape Girardeau

Afterwards Mrs. Harvey proceeded to Cape Girardeau, where hospitals were being improvised for the immediate

---
[1] Love, p. 1045.

WISCONSIN WOMEN IN THE WAR

use of the sick and dying, then being brought in from the swamps by the returning regiments, and up the rivers in closely-crowded hospital boats. These hospitals were mere sheds filled with cots, side by side; so close, there was scarcely room for a person to pass between them. Mrs. Harvey describes their conditions as follows:

Pneumonia, typhoid, and camp fevers, and that fearful scourge of the Southern swamps and rivers, chronic diarrhoea, occupied every bed. A surgeon once said to me, "There is nothing else there; here I see pneumonia, and there fever, and on that cot another disease, and I see nothing else! You had better stay away; the air is full of contagion; and contagion and sympathy dc not go well together."

One day a woman passed through these uncomfortable, ill-ventilated, hot, unclean, infected, wretched rooms; and *she* saw something else there. A hand reached out and clutched her dress. One caught her shawl and kissed it, another her hand, and pressed it to his fevered cheek; another in wild delirium cried, "I want to go home! I want to go home! Lady! Lady! Take me in your chariot; take me away!" * * *

This woman failed to see on these cots aught but the human [beings] they were to her; the sons, brothers, husbands, and fathers of anxious weeping ones at home, and as such she cared for, and thought of them. Arm in arm with health, she visited day by day every sufferer's cot, doing, it is true, very little, but always taking with her from the outside world fresh air, fresh flowers, and all the hope and comfort she could find in her heart to give them. [2]

Although Mrs. Harvey speaks thus modestly of her labors at Cape Girardeau, her work there was really heroic, for the conditions with which she had to contend were more distressing than can be described. In the intensely

---

[2] Ms. lecture by Mrs. Harvey, loaned to the author by Mrs. James Selkirk of Clinton.

MRS. HARVEY

warm climate, contagious diseases flourished. Mrs. Harvey found on her arrival that the body of a dead soldier had lain for hours unattended to, because those in charge were afraid to touch it. But Mrs. Harvey was not afraid; with her own hands she bound up the face, and encouraged by her coolness the burial party was induced to coffin the body and remove it from the house.[3]

Secures Reforms

Worse than all was the fact that the sick and wounded had nothing to subsist on but the common army rations. One of Mrs. Harvey's first acts was to telegraph to the president of the Western Sanitary Commission for hospital stores; such were sent immediately to her in liberal measure.[4] Soon after returning to St. Louis, Mrs. Harvey came back to Wisconsin, where she did much to arouse enthusiasm among the women and to give direction to their work. In October she again revisted the hospitals, where she did all in her power to comfort the soldiers by writing to their friends and procuring discharges for those who were unfit for service. She returned to St. Louis on November 1, when the surgeon in charge of the hospitals wrote to Governor Salomon, commending her efforts. During the same month General Curtis gave her permission to visit all the hospitals in his command, and he sent orders to quartermasters and transportation companies to afford her and her sanitary articles free transmission. So she started on a tour of inspection, which embraced all the general hospitals on the Mississippi River as well as the

---

[3] Brockett, p. 263.
[4] *Ibid*, p. 264.

regimental hospitals for Wisconsin soldiers. On this tour she visited those at Helena, St. Louis, Rolla, Ironton, and Memphis.[5]

While on a steamer from Cape Girardeau to Helena, Mrs. Harvey heard a young major in the regular army coolly remarked that it was much cheaper for the Government to keep her sick soldiers in hospitals on the river, than to furlough them. Upon which she quietly remarked:

"That is true, Major, if all were faithful to the Government, but unfortunately a majority of the surgeons in the army have conscientious scruples, and verily believe it to be their duty to keep these sick men alive as long as possible. * * * Don't you think, sir, that it would be a trifle more economical to send these poor fellows North for a few weeks, to regain their strength, that they might return at once to active service?"

Mrs. Harvey was prevented from hearing the Major's reply on account of the other officers' laughter. It seems that the Major was the medical director at Helena, where over 2,000 Northern soldiers lay buried. It was Mrs. Harvey's opinion that two-thirds of these men might have been saved if they had been sent North. Upon inquiry she learned from the surgeon in charge of the hospital that he had several times made out certificates of disability in order to secure furloughs for some of the men in his hospital; but when these were sent to the medical director for his signature, they had been invariably disapproved. He had also permitted the men to submit their papers in person; only to have them severely reproved, and ordered back by the director, "and," he continued with tears in

---

[5] *Ibid*, p. 264; Tuttle, p. 701.

MRS. HARVEY

his eyes, "many of them never returned, for broken-hearted, they have lain down by the roadside and died."[6]

Influence with Officials

Mrs. Harvey had one memorable experience in securing the discharge of a sick boy. His mother had succeeded in getting her son as far as St. Louis, where his papers were to be sent; but here she met with reverses, for the papers sent to the medical director were improperly made out, consequently his approval was not secured. The broken-hearted mother told her story to Mrs. Harvey that same night. She impulsively said, "Give me the papers," and off she went to the office of the medical director. "He was a man fully six feet high, over fifty years of age, [with] a beard like Oliver Cromwell's, a face as stern as fate, and of the regular army." She entered his office, seated herself and waited till he spoke to her. After a curt question or two the general went on writing; finally he turned and said: "May as well hear it now as ever, what is it?" Whereupon Mrs. Harvey stated the case as well as she could, interrupted only by the half-rude, half-impatient remarks of the inspector. Finally he said, as if in self-defense, "We have army regulations; we cannot go behind them. You know, if I do, they will rap me over the knuckles at Washington." To this the quick-witted, earnest little woman replied, "Oh, that your knuckles were mine. I would be willing to have them skinned; the skin will grow again you know."

"Where are these papers?" he said sharply. "I have them here in my pocket." "Let me see them." Mrs. Har-

---

[6] Harvey Ms., p. 3.

WISCONSIN WOMEN IN THE WAR

vey took them out slowly and handed them over to him, blank side up. He turned them, and his face flushed as he said, "Why I have had these papers and disapproved them. This is my signature." Tremblingly she replied, "I knew it, but forgive me. I thought maybe when you knew about it, General, and the mother was weeping with the skeleton arms of the boy around her neck—I thought maybe you would do something or tell me something to do." "Suppose I do approve these papers, it will do no good. The general in command will stop them and censure me." "But you will have done all you could and have obeyed the higher law."

She had won, for the remorseful man crossed out with a firm stroke of his pen "disapproved," and wrote "approved" upon the discharge, after which he said in a quick, husky tone, "Take it, and don't you come here again today." As Mrs. Harvey raised her eyes to thank him, she saw a scowl on his brow, a smile on his lips, but tears in his eyes.[7]

Another story shows how Mrs. Harvey succeeded in securing the assistance she wanted. An erring boy of nineteen had deserted from a Minnesota regiment; later he had joined a Wisconsin regiment, from which he had been honorably discharged after having been wounded in a battle. In one of the lowest dens in St. Louis he had been drugged, robbed, and left lying on a filthy mattress. There he was found tossing from side to side, stricken by disease and in a delirious condition. Mrs. Harvey soothed him as best she could. Recognizing the hand of kindness on his burning brow, he cried "Mother." After a touch-

---

[7] *Ibid*, pp. 4, 5.

MRS. HARVEY

ing scene she left, promising to return in half an hour and take him away. This was easier said than done; the boy was at that time only a citizen and not a soldier, and therefore he could not be admitted to a military hospital. But he was dying, and in order to prevent his mother from knowing that he had died in such a place, Mrs. Harvey determined to make a desperate effort to get him admitted to the hospital.

So she went to her old friend the medical director, and told her story, saying, "General, write an order quick to the surgeon in charge of the Fifth Street hospital, that the boy may be received. I also want an ambulance, mattress, and bedding, and some men to help me to move him." "Yes, yes, but listen, I have no right; I can't do it." "I know—I know, but please do hurry—I promised to be back in half an hour, and the boy will expect me." The General imitating her voice, gave the order and continued, "Here is the paper; what else do you want? Henceforth we do what you wish and no questions asked. It is the easiest way and I guess the only way to get along with you."[8]

At Memphis

Early in February, 1863, Mrs. Harvey went to Memphis, from which place she sent a letter to the Governor of our State urging him to establish a hospital at that place. Here she also succeeded in procuring furloughs for men who would otherwise have died. In fact, her influence was so great that the poor and ignorant ones had a strange, almost superstitious reverence for her as one who used her

[8] *Ibid*, p. 6.

WISCONSIN WOMEN IN THE WAR

great power for the good of the common soldier.[9] The estimate formed of her authority by some of the more ignorant class showed itself sometimes in a ludicrous manner. For instance she received letters from homesick men, begging her to give them a furlough in order to visit their families; even deserters and men confined in military prisons, asked her to help them and set them at liberty, promising her that they would reform.[10]

A Wisconsin soldier who had been left in a convalescent camp at Memphis, gives a glimpse of Mrs. Harvey at her labors. He saw her at the camp several times, carrying fruits and wine in a basket; he saw her also at the general hospital, where she again carried her basket, full of delicacies. When the soldiers heard she was in the room, they used to raise themselves from their pillows and call her the "Wisconsin Angel." Each Wisconsin soldier received a treat from the basket, and Mrs. Harvey was sorry when she was unable to dispense her charity to all the Union soldiers in the hospital.

There was a surgeon from Wisconsin at this same hospital, who was proving untrustworthy on account of his fondness for drink; Mrs. Harvey was determined to have him removed. She sent for him to come to see her and informed him that she had written to the authorities at Madison, and that he was to leave at once, as he was unfit for duty.[11]

---

[9] Tuttle, p. 701.
[10] Brockett, p. 265.
[11] Ms. letter of G. H. McIntyre (Portage, April 2, 1910).

MRS. HARVEY

Brings Sick Soldiers to the North

After visiting Memphis, Mrs. Harvey inspected hospitals at Corinth, Jackson, and La Grange. She met General Grant at Vicksburg in March, 1863; here she succeeded finally in securing from him an order that patients who suffered from chronic dysentery should be sent to Northern hospitals, and that the convalescent camp at Memphis should be cleared out by discharging the men who were unfit for service, and by sending others to their regiments; that medical inspectors should be appointed for every army corps, and that they should have full power to discharge disabled men. [12]

Mrs. Harvey began her task at Memphis, where she found 100 men in a convalescent camp at Fort Pickering. These men could not live unless they were taken North. She accompanied them up the river to Cairo; from there they went by rail to St. Louis, where a transport awaited them. In the meantime Mrs. Harvey had not only secured transportation for them to Madison, but as they were needy and had not been paid, she procured a change of clothing for each one from the Western Sanitary Commission. The experiment was a success, for out of the whole number released from this camp only seven died. [13]

Inspects Hospitals

In the spring of 1863, General Grant was making his approaches upon Vicksburg. At that time Young's Point, across the river, was the limit of uninterrupted navigation,

---
[12] Tuttle, p. 701.
[13] Brockett, p. 266.

and there much sickness existed caused by the high water covering the low lands. About April 1, Mrs. Harvey began her work at this point, but after a few weeks she was overcome by the miasma, and was obliged to return to the North, where after a few months of rest in New York and Wisconsin, she recovered her health.[14] It was on her return trip from the North that she visited Washington and obtained from President Lincoln permission to establish a hospital in Wisconsin for convalescent soldiers.[15]

Returning to the South Mrs. Harvey again visited all of the hospitals on the river, down as far as New Orleans, making Vicksburg the centre of her field of labor. Here her presence was in itself a power for good, so great was the reputation she had won in the army. Hospital officers and attendants were especially affected by her return; they knew how quickly she would find out and condemn any delinquency on their part, and they acted accordingly. During the summer of 1864, the garrison at Vicksburg suffered intensely from various diseases; the mortality was especially great among the men of the Second Wisconsin Cavalry. "Strong men sickened and died within a few days, others lingered for weeks, wasting by degrees, till only skin and bone were left.[16] The survivors, as evidence of their appreciation of the services of Mrs. Harvey, presented her with an enamelled watch, set with diamonds. She disliked a presentation ceremony, but could not avoid it in this case; those present must have been astonished

---

[14] Tuttle, p. 701.
[15] See succeeding chapter.
[16] Brockett, p. 267.

MRS. HARVEY

when observing the poor appearance she made in public. For this woman, who was "resolute, impetuous, confident to a degree, bordering on the imperious, with power of denunciation to equip an orator," seemed to lose all her power of effective speech on this occasion, and to be quite overcome by her feelings.

Although Mrs. Harvey was the sanitary agent for Wisconsin, she paid little regard to state lines, and her work may truly be regarded as national. Wisconsin citizens consider her as the highest embodiment of womanly helpfulness and virtue which our State produced during the Civil War period.

Chapter IX

Mrs. Harvey's Interview with Lincoln

Throughout Mrs. Harvey's narrative of her experiences in the early years of the war, runs a thread of criticism of existing conditions, especially of that military regulation which kept sick soldiers in Southern hospitals instead of sending them North, where the bracing atmosphere might restore them to health. To her the idea of military hospitals in the North seemed eminently practicable, and she could see no reason why the authorities should oppose such a project. She was not the only one who tried to secure such an arrangement; Governor Salomon had from the beginning of his term of office done everything in his power to further this matter, but his efforts were of no avail.[17] Finally Mrs. Harvey and Mrs. Eliza Porter proposed to Senator Howe that he draw up a petition praying for the establishment of such hospitals. This was done, and through the efforts of these two women and other friends of the enterprise, eight thousand signatures were secured.[18] It was then proposed that Mrs. Porter should take the petition to Washington, for as Mrs. Harvey said:

By sending it * * * by this officer and that one, we began to feel that the message lost the flavor of the truth and got cold,

---

[17] Quiner, p. 158.
[18] Brockett, p. 164.

MRS. HARVEY AND LINCOLN

before it reached the deciding power, and because it was so lukewarm, he spued it out of his mouth. It is always best, if you wish to secure an object * * * to go at once to the highest power, be your own petitioner, in temporal as in spiritual matters, officiate at your own altar, be your own priest.[19]

Seeing the President

Mrs. Porter having refused to be the bearer of the petition, Mrs. Harvey went instead:

By the advice of friends, and with the intense feeling that something must be done I went to Washington. I entered the White House, not with fear and trembling, but strong and self possessed, fully conscious of the righteousness of my mission.

* * * * * * * *

When I first saw him [President Lincoln] his head was bent forward, his chin resting on his breast, and in his hand a letter, which I had just sent in to him. He raised his eyes, saying, "Mrs. Harvey." I hastened forward, and replied, "Yes, and I am glad to see you, Mr. Lincoln!" So much for Republican presentation and ceremony. The President took my hand, hoped I was well, but there was no smile of welcome on his face. It was rather the stern look of the judge, who had decided against me. His face was peculiar—bone, nerve, vein, and muscle were all so plainly seen; deep lines of thought and care were around his mouth and eyes. The word justice came into my mind, as though I could read it upon his face—I mean, that extended sense of the word, that comprehends the practice of every virtue which reason prescribes and society should expect. The debt we owe to God, to man, to ourselves, when paid is but a simple act of justice, a duty performed. This attribute seemed the source of Mr. Lincoln's strength.

After he had read the paper introducing Mrs. Harvey

---

[19] Harvey Ms., pp. 7, 8.

and her mission, he looked at her with a good deal of sad severity and said:

"Madam, this matter of Northern hospitals has been talked of a great deal, and I thought it was settled; but it seems not. What have you got to say about it?" "Only this, Mr. Lincoln, that many soldiers in our Western army, on the Mississippi River, *must* have Northern air or die. There are thousands of graves all along our Southern rivers, and in the swamps, for which the Government is responsible; ignorantly, undoubtedly, but this ignorance must not continue. If you will permit these men to come North, you will have ten men where you have one now.

The President could not comprehend this forceful argument; he could not understand that by sending one sick man to the North, this North would produce in a year ten healthy men. Mrs. Harvey made her point clear, but Lincoln answered: "Yes, yes, I understand you; but if they are sent North, they will desert; where is the difference?" "Dead men cannot fight, and they may not desert," she answered.

Interview with Stanton

Thus the war of argument ran on, Mrs. Harvey valiantly defending her position, the President attacking it. Finally both parties to the debate realized that they had reached a deadlock, and Mr. Lincoln said: "Well, well, Mrs. Harvey, you go and see the Secretary of War and talk with him, and hear what he has to say."

I left him for the War Department. I found written on the back of the letter these words, "Admit Mrs. Harvey at once; listen to what she says; she is a lady of intelligence and talks sense. A. LINCOLN."

MRS. HARVEY AND LINCOLN

Not displeased with this introduction Mrs. Harvey went to see the Secretary of War, who informed her that he had sent the Surgeon-General to New Orleans on a tour of hospital inspection. Mrs. Harvey knew that this procedure would practically have no effect on existing conditions, whereupon she replied, "The truth is, the medical authorities know the heads of departments do not wish hospitals established so far away from army lines, and report accordingly. I wish this could be overruled; can nothing be done?" "Nothing until the Surgeon-General returns," Mr. Stanton replied. So the valiant woman left him, not at all disappointed with her day's work, because she felt that she had made a deep impression on both these earnest and conscientious men, and could afford to wait for the result of her interviews. On that memorable day she met a friend in the street, who said to her, "How long are you going to stay here?" "Until I get what I came after." "That's right, that's right; go on; I believe in the final perseverance of the saints."

The President Unconvinced

The next morning she returned to the White House full of hope, but no smile greeted her. The President had been annoyed and worried by a woman pleading for the life of her son, and was not the genial, open-minded man he had been the night before. Mrs. Harvey relates her interview as follows:

After a moment he said, "Well," with a peculiar contortion of the face, I never saw in any one else. I replied, "Well," and he looked at me a little astonished, I fancied, and said, "Have you nothing to say?" "Nothing, Mr. President, until I hear your decision. You bade me come this morning; have you decided?"

WISCONSIN WOMEN IN THE WAR

"No, but I believe this idea of Northern hospitals is a great humbug, and I am tired of hearing about it." He spoke impatiently. I replied, "I regret to add a feather's weight to your already overwhelming care and responsibility. I would rather have stayed at home." With a kind of half smile, he said, "I wish you had." I answered him as though he had not smiled, "Nothing would have given me greater pleasure; but a keen sense of duty to this Government, justice and mercy to its most loyal supporters, and regard for your honor and position made me come. The people cannot understand why their friends are left to die, when with proper care they might live and do good service for their country. * * *

"Many on their cots, faint, sick and dying say, 'We would gladly do more, but suppose that it is all right.' I know that the majority of them would live and be strong men again, if they could be sent North. I say, I know, because I was sick among them last spring; surrounded by every comfort, with the best of care, and determined to get well. I grew weaker, day by day, until not being under military law, my friends brought me North. I recovered entirely, simply by breathing the Northern air."

While I was speaking the expression of Mr. Lincoln's face had changed many times. He had never taken his eyes from me. Now every muscle of his face seemed to contract, and then suddenly expand. As he opened his mouth, you could almost hear them snap, as he said, "You assume to know more than I do," and closed his mouth as though he never expected to open it again, sort of slammed it to; I could scarcely reply. I was hurt and thought the tears would come, but rallied in a moment and said, "You must pardon me, Mr. President, I intend no disrespect, but it is because of this knowledge—because I do know, what you do not know, that I come to you. If you knew what I do, and had not ordered what I ask for, I should know that an appeal to you would be vain; but I believe that the people have not trusted you for naught. The question only is, whether you believe me or not. If you believe me, you will give me hospitals;

MRS. HARVEY AND LINCOLN

if not, not." With the same snapping of muscle, he again said, "You assume to know more than surgeons do."

To this Mrs. Harvey replied, that the medical authorities knew that Lincoln was opposed to establishing hospitals in the North, and that they reported so as to please him, and she continued:

"I come to you from no casual tour of inspection passing rapidly through the general hospitals, * * * with a cigar in my mouth, and a rattan in my hand, talking to the surgeon-in-charge of the price of cotton, and abusing the generals in our army for not knowing and performing their duty better, and finally coming into the open air, with a long-drawn breath as though they had just escaped suffocation, and complacently saying, 'You have a very fine hospital here; the boys seem to be doing very well, a little more attention to ventilation is perhaps desirable.'

"It is not thus I have visited hospitals; but from early morning until late at night sometimes, I have visited the regimental and general hospitals on the Mississippi River from Quincy to Vicksburg, and I come to you from the cots of men who have died, who might have lived had you permitted. This is hard to say, but it is none the less true." During the time that I had been speaking Mr. Lincoln's brow had become very much contracted, and a severe scowl had settled over his whole face. He sharply asked, how many men Wisconsin had in the field; that is, how many did she send. I replied, "About fifty thousand, I think. I do not know exactly." "That means, she has about twenty thousand now." He looked at me, and said, "You need not look so sober, they are not all dead." I did not reply.

After some conversation of a more general nature Mrs. Harvey left the President with the understanding that she would receive her answer at twelve the next day.

WISCONSIN WOMEN IN THE WAR

Mrs. Harvey Successful

The next morning she arose with a terribly depressed feeling that perhaps she would fail in her great mission. She was nervous and impatient and found herself looking at her watch, and wondering if twelve o'clock would never come. Finally she went to the White House, where she was informed by a messenger that a cabinet meeting was in session, and that she was to await the adjournment. After three hours, during which she felt more and more certain of defeat, Mr. Lincoln came into the room where she was waiting. He came forward, rubbing his hands and saying, "My dear Madam, I am very sorry to have kept you waiting. We have but this moment adjourned." She replied, "My waiting is no matter, but you must be very tired, and we will not talk tonight." But the President asked her to sit down and said, "Mrs. Harvey, I only wish to tell you, that an order equivalent to granting a hospital in your State has been issued nearly twenty-four hours." Let Mrs. Harvey continue the story in her own words:

I could not speak, I was so entirely unprepared for it. I wept for joy, I could not help it. When I could speak I said, "God bless you! I thank you in the name of thousands, who will bless you for the act." * * * I was so much agitated, I could not talk with him. He noticed it and commenced talking upon other subjects * * *

I shortly after left with the promise to call next morning, as he desired me to do at nine o'clock. I suppose the excitement caused the intense suffering of that night. I was very ill, and it was ten o'clock the next morning before I was able to send for a carriage to keep my appointment with the President.

MRS. HARVEY AND LINCOLN

More than fifty people were in the waiting room, so Mrs. Harvey turned to go; but a voice said, "Mrs. Harvey, the President will see you now." As she passed through the crowd, one person said, "She has been here every day and what is more, she is going to win." Mr. Lincoln greeted her cordially and gave her a copy of the order he had just issued. She thanked him for it and apologized to being late, whereupon he asked, "Did joy make you sick?" to which she answered, "I don't know, very likely it was the relaxation of nerve after intense excitement." Still looking at her he said, "I suppose you would have been mad if I had said 'no'?" "No, Mr. Lincoln, I should neither have been angry nor sick." "What would you have done?" he asked curiously. "I should have been here at nine o'clock, Mr. President." "Well," he laughingly said, "I think I acted wisely then. Don't you ever get angry?" he asked. "I know a little woman, not very unlike you, who gets mad sometimes." Mrs. Harvey answered, "I never get angry, when I have an object to gain of the importance of the one under consideration; to get angry, you know, would only weaken my cause and destroy my influence." "That is true, that is true," he said decidedly. "This hospital I shall name for you." But Mrs. Harvey said modestly, "If you would not consider the request indelicate, I would like to have it named for Mr. Harvey." "Yes, just as well, it shall be so understood, if you prefer it. I honored your husband and felt his loss." After some further conversation Mr. Lincoln looked at her from under his eyebrows and said, "You almost think me handsome, don't you?" His face then beamed with such kind benevolence, and was lighted

WISCONSIN WOMEN IN THE WAR

by such a pleasant smile, that she looked at him and said impulsively, "You are perfectly lovely to me now, Mr Lincoln," at which he blushed a little, and laughed most heartily.

As she arose to go, he reached out his hand—that hand in which there was so much power and little beauty— and hold hers clasped and covered in his own. Mrs. Harvey relates further:

> I bowed my head and pressed my lips most reverently upon the sacred shield, even as I would upon my country's shrine. A silent prayer went up from my heart, "God bless you, Abraham Lincoln!" I heard him say goodbye, and I was gone. Thus ended the most interesting interview of my life, with one of the most remarkable men of the age.
>
> My impressions of him had been so varied, his character had assumed so many different phases, his very looks had changed so frequently, and so entirely, that it almost seemed to me I had been conversing with half a dozen different men. He blended in his character the most yielding flexibility with the most unflinching firmness; child-like simplicity and weakness, with statesman-like wisdom and masterly strength; but over and around all was thrown the mantle of an unquestioned integrity. [20]

It is almost superfluous to comment upon Mrs. Harvey's part in these memorable interviews, for the reader of her descriptions cannot but feel her power and strength of character. She was like a wise general who is not overconfident by apparent success, nor unduly depressed by apparent defeat. Moreover, in her was united a masculine grasp of a situation and a remarkable power of argument,

---

[20] The source of this entire account is the Harvey manuscript, pp. 9–19.

MRS. HARVEY AND LINCOLN

with womanly tact and patience, which finally secured the victory. Wisconsin people may feel that in this interview with Abraham Lincoln, Mrs. Harvey rose to the situation with a greatness not below that of the President, whom she so truly called "one of the most remarkable men of the age."

Northern Hospitals

As a result of Mrs. Harvey's intercession with President Lincoln, three convalescent camps or hospitals were established in Wisconsin—at Madison, at Milwaukee, and at Prairie du Chien.[21] The Harvey United States Army General Hospital, as it was called, was established at Madison in October, 1863. After several buildings were examined, the Farwell house was chosen, a three-storied octagonal building near Lake Monona. Within a month Dr. Howard Culbertson was placed at his head, and his conduct of the institution was thus endorsed by Surgeon-General Wolcott:

I have frequently visited the Harvey Hospital, and it affords me great pleasure to bear testimony to the untiring zeal and ability of the Surgeon in charge, and the medical officers and subordinates under him. The essential excellence of a Hospital consists in the successful results of efforts to restore the inmates to health, or the nearest approximation to it, if possible. The general policy, hygienic regulations, orders, rules, etc., should all tend to this grand result. Viewed in this light, although there are many much more spacious and commodious hospitals in the country, very few will be found superior to the Harvey Hospital. Remediable cases, whether requiring surgical or medicinal means or both, are seasonably and skilfully treated. * * * Those of our gallant sick and wounded boys,

---

[21] R. G. Thwaites, *Wisconsin* (Boston, 1909), p. 345.

who are so fortunate as to be inmates of the Harvey Hospital, have abundant reason for self-gratulation. Of such there are at this time about 630, including those at the Branch, Camp Randall. [22]

This admirably-conducted institution was in operation until the close of the war, when it was discontinued—its patients either discharged, or transferred to the Post Hospital at Camp Randall. The hospitals at Milwaukee and Prairie du Chien were established in 1864, the former being designed as an officers' hospital. The one at Prairie du Chien was known as the Swift Hospital; its buildings are now a part of the Sacred Heart Academy. There were five wards in its main building, and four regular nurses. As far as can be learned it was well managed. [23]

Soldiers' Orphans' Home

During the last two years of the war Mrs. Harvey had been considering the establishment of a home in Wisconsin for the orphans of soldiers. When she returned from the South in 1865, she brought with her six or seven orphans of the war, whom she had found there, not inquiring on which side their fathers fought. [24] Having learned that the Government was about to discontinue the several hospitals in the Northern states, she thought the Harvey Hospital so well adapted for an orphanage, that negotiations were at once begun with the owners of the property. So liberal was the offer made by them, that Governor

---

[22] Surgeon General's *Report*, 1864, in *Governor's Message and Documents* (Madison, 1865), p. 965.

[23] Ms. letter of Edward Rittenhouse (Monona, Iowa).

[24] Anna B. Butler, editor, *Centennial Records of Women of Wisconsin* (Madison, 1876), p. 38.

THE WISCONSIN SOLDIERS' ORPHANS' HOME, AT MADISON
From a contemporary photograph in possession of the Wisconsin Historical Society

MRS. HARVEY AND LINCOLN

Lewis decided to send Mrs. Harvey to Washington in order to secure a title to the three wings that had been erected by the United States. The War Department had no authority to make such a donation, but upon investigation it was ascertained that these additions when torn down would have no value to the Government except as old lumber. An arrangement was thereupon made, by which the proprietors received the buildings in lieu of rent and repairs, on condition that the property should be used as a home for soldiers' orphans.

Through the generosity of interested friends in Madison and other places the property was purchased for such a home. Repairs were immediately begun, and the building was ready by January 1, 1866, to receive soldiers' orphans. The personal exertions of Mrs. Harvey and the liberality of her friends, thus resulted in starting a charitable enterprise which was conducted as a private institution until March 31, 1866, when its maintenance was assumed by the State.

The building contained dormitories, sleeping rooms, a school-room capable of seating 150 children, an infirmary, and a sewing-room. In April, 1866, the home housed eighty-five children with Mrs. Harvey in charge. As superintendent, she was "the chief executive officer of the home, to have control and authority over all assistants connected with the institution below the grade designated in the by-laws as officers; to employ or discharge as [she] may see fit, being responsible to the trustees for the proper discharge of that duty." [25]

The qualifications for admission to the institution were: "All orphans over the age of four and under fourteen

---

[25] Quiner, pp. 12–15.

WISCONSIN WOMEN IN THE WAR

years, whose fathers enlisted from the State, and who have either been killed or died while in the military or naval services of the United States, or of this State, during the late rebellion, or who have since died of diseases contracted while in such service, and who have no means of support, shall be entitled to the benefits of this institution, giving the preference to those having neither father nor mother, in deciding upon applications."

During the year that Mrs. Harvey was superintendent the institution was well established. She gave personal supervision to even the smallest details and took the trouble to learn the name of every child, although their number soon increased to 300. In May, 1867, she resigned, and from that time on the office of superintendent was filled by men whose wives acted as matrons, giving in all instances "their whole strength and energy and tenderest care to their work."[26] Women were always employed as teachers, and regarded their task as a labor of love, in which no effort was spared to supply the place of real mothers to the children.

In 1872 Mr. and Mrs. R. W. Burton became superintendent and matron respectively. By this time some of the girls were approaching womanhood, and Mrs. Burton, like her predecessor, spared no pains in surrounding the children with elevating and refining influences. Many of the children having grown up and gone out from the home to find their places in society, the State in 1874, feeling the need for retrenchment, closed the institution.[27]

---

[26] *Centennial Records*, p. 39.

[27] May 29, 1908, on the Madison site of this hospital and orphans' home a tablet was erected, the gift of the school children of the city, who attended the exercises in large numbers, and took part in the patriotic songs. An oration was delivered by

MRS. HARVEY AND LINCOLN

The home was exceedingly well managed during its entire eight years' existence; the sanitary condition was excellent, so that during the whole period but eight deaths occurred. There were often as many as 300 children residing within its walls, whose training, both in school work and in domestic science, was effective. Many of those who left the home became teachers, or entered higher schools for further study. The State supported the institution generously by an annual grant of $25,000; and both the State authorities and the officials of the home made a special effort to impress on the children that it was not a charitable institution, but was accorded to them as a debt of gratitude by the State for the loss of their fathers. [28]

The establishment of the Wisconsin Soldiers' Orphans' Home was a part of a national movement in the direction of such charities. Toward the close of the war soldiers' homes, soldiers' orphans' homes, pensions for veterans, and employment of veterans in the civil service, became important subjects in the public mind. The need for soldiers' orphan asylums was urged throughout the country, and many such state and local institutions were erected. [29]

Attorney-General Frank L. Gilbert, who had himself been one of the boys reared in the home. The tablet reads: "On this city block, during the Civil War, stood Harvey Hospital, and later the Wisconsin Soldiers' Orphans' Home, both established through the influence of Mrs. Harvey, whose honored husband, Governor Louis P. Harvey, had accidentally been drowned in Tennessee River, near Shiloh battlefield, April 19, 1862, where he had gone after the battle, with supplies for the comfort of the sick and wounded Wisconsin soldiers."

[28] Ms. letter of Mary E. Skinner (Seattle, Wash., May 5, 1910).
[29] Fite, pp. 286, 287.

Chapter X

The Christian Commission

"The United States Christian Commission, while not neglecting the physical and material wants of the soldiers, had for its primary object their spiritual welfare, just as the Sanitary Commission attended mainly to the physical, though not entirely neglecting the spiritual."[30]

The Christian Commission was organized on November 14, 1861, at New York City; its primary purpose was to supplement the work of chaplains in the army by sending ministers and delegates to the field. It distributed to the soliders Bibles, tracts, hymn-books, and literature of all sorts. In course of time its operations became more and more of a sanitary character, as it maintained special diet kitchens, where a "gospel of suitable and delicate food was administered with Christian kindness."[31] The Commission also tried to find employment for returning soldiers. But its main interest was a spiritual one, for it "aided the surgeon, helped the chaplain, followed the armies in their marches, went into trenches and along the picket-line. Wherever there was a sick, a wounded, a dying man, an agent of the Christian Commission was near by. Moreover, it arranged Christian burials, whenever possi-

---

[30] *Ibid*, p. 284.
[31] Moore, p. 579.

THE CHRISTIAN COMMISSION

ble, marked the graves of the dead, held religious services in extemporized chapels, and conducted prayer-meetings. [32]

Religious Awakening

During the first two years of the war the Commission did not receive the full support of the general public, consequently its means were limited and its efficiency correspondingly feeble; but by 1863 the attitude of the public began to change, and quite suddenly the Commission found itself a power. In the summer of 1863, the religious life of the people began to be quickened. There were revival meetings and activity in building new churches everywhere. In fact, there was a reaction from the feelings at first inspired by the war. A recent writer says:

The first blows of fighting had stunned man's sensibilities; hospitals filled with the wounded, countless funerals at one's very door, the anguish and the suffering, at first filled men with that feeling which has been voiced by the present generation in the cry, "Remember the Maine." It was then: "Remember Colonel Ellsworth," "Remember my son," the utterance of a spirit of revenge, that plainly was not compatible with a spirit of prayer. [33]

This change took place gradually, without excitement or hysteria, for it was a natural reaction from the awful experiences of the first two years of the war. Along with the revival in religion came an increased interest in charities of all sorts, and the Christian Commission reaped the benefit of this new missionary spirit.

---

[32] J. W. Draper, *Civil War in America* (New York, 1867), iii, pp. 519, 520.

[33] Fite, pp. 306-310.

WISCONSIN WOMEN IN THE WAR

Women's Auxiliaries

Up to 1864 the women of the North did not take any active part in the Christian Commission. On May 4 of that year a meeting of women was held at Philadelphia for the purpose of organizing Ladies' Christian Commissions in the various churches throughout the country. These were to be auxiliary to the United States Commission. Any member of a congregation could become a member of the Commission by paying one dollar a year, which fee was to be paid over to the United States Commission for a national membership fund. All money left, after the necessary expenses were paid, was to be turned over to another national fund, known as the Donation Fund.[34] This movement was national, and affected Wisconsin women as well as those of other states.

Wisconsin Commission

Until 1864 the people of Wisconsin sent their contributions to the Chicago Branch of the Christian Commission, for there was no Wisconsin organization before that date. On October 8, 1864, Walter S. Carter of Milwaukee organized the Wisconsin Branch, which seems to have been very successful, for between the date of its organization and July, 1865, it received from the various churches of the State $8,868. The largest single contribution came from Fond du Lac, where nearly $1,400 was contributed at a single collection. The Wisconsin Branch's contribution of stores was also heavy, exceeding that of all other branches

---

[34] *Ladies' Christian Commissions Auxiliary to U. S. Christian Commission* (Philadelphia, 1864).

THE CHRISTIAN COMMISSION

except Pittsburg and Cincinnati. The total number of packages from Wisconsin was 1,048, the value of which was estimated at $54,915. One donation made to eleven Wisconsin regiments at Mobile, amounted to more than 450 barrels, including forty barrels of pickles and more than three tons of dried apples. The Wisconsin Branch also sent forty-five delegates to the field, a larger number than those of any other branch during the same period, except Boston, Cincinnati, Brooklyn, and Chicago. The total amount received by the Wisconsin Branch during the nine months of its existence was $63,883.87. Concerning the work of the Wisconsin Commission it is asserted:

> If to this sum were added the value of the delegates' services, and of railroad and telegraph facilities, the amount would exceed seventy-five thousand dollars. And all this was the spontaneous gift of the people; the Branch not having a single salaried officer or employee, and its entire expenses, from its organization to its close, being but $1,743.38, or only about two per cent of its receipts. [35]

Experiences of Wisconsin Women

The experiences of Mrs. Mary Burnell Robinson in the Christian Commission work are worth recording. A relative of hers, Rev. K. A. Burnell, was in charge of the Department of Mississippi, with headquarters at Memphis. It was through his influence, that women's work under the Commission's auspices began. In 1862 he obtained permission to appoint as his assistants two women of his family, who remained in the South until 1865. One of the sisters "found her favorite work in the freedmen's schools, then being established;" the other was the libra-

---
[35] Love, pp. 1052, 1053.

WISCONSIN WOMEN IN THE WAR

rian of the Commission's reading-room in Memphis. This room was located in a store under the Gayoso House, at that time the largest hotel in the city. The apartment was large and had a beautiful view of the river from its windows; it contained a library of two hundred volumes, newspaper files, and other reading matter, and a long writing-table, on which was spread free stationery. There was also an organ in the room, used for religious services, which were conducted during the afternoons. Mrs. Robinson writes of these meetings as follows:

> It was then that our organ came into use, and much good singing was had, I being the happy accompanist. These meetings were ever a joy to the Christian soldiers, who had oftentimes very little to help them to the spiritual life. Many who had already blackslidden were restored and others converted. It is hardly necessary to say, that our position there gave us a great opportunity to talk with them, and as a rule they were frank and confiding—glad of any help. Often, too, we wrote letters for them, where they had given up for us their right hand or arm or were temporarily disabled, and all these things made a way to their hearts, which we tried to make a highway for the Lord. [36]

Other Wisconsin women who served as delegates for the Christian Commission, were Miss Katherine Bissell of Delavan, who had charge of the Commission rooms at Little Rock; and Mrs. Annie Johnson Ensign, who had charge of the field-work between Cairo and Vicksburg, and whose duty it was to meet soldiers returning from the field of battle. [37]

---

[36] Ms. letter of Mrs. Mary Burnell Robinson (Topeka, Kans., May 17, 1910).

[37] Ms. letter of Mrs. Ensign (Boise, Idaho, May 27, 1910).

THE CHRISTIAN COMMISSION

Reading Material

From the beginning of the war the volunteers manifested a lively interest in the reading matter which the Commission endeavored to provide for them. One wrote:

Cannot there be some means devised, by which a greater supply of reading can be supplied to the men in the army? There would be a vast deal less of drinking and swearing among the men if a sufficiency of reading, such as newspapers, historical works, and magazines could be had. * * * It is but a trifling task to wrap up a paper, after you have perused it, and send it to some friend in the army. There are young ladies enough, who I presume would willingly devote two or three hours each day in gathering up, from house to house, newspapers, books, magazines, etc., if they only knew how much it would please their soldier friends. * * * We hope, that in every city and town in Wisconsin, a society the object of which shall be to furnish reading for our soldiers, will be organized, and the worthy cause commenced at once. Who will make the first move? [38]

Madison women were among those who made the first move in this direction and aroused much enthusiasm by so doing. Acknowledging this fact a writer says:

God bless the patriotic ladies of Madison for their generous sympathy in behalf of the citizen-soldiers * * * in collecting papers and other good reading matter, that shall make their stay in Camp Randall pleasant and morally profitable. * * * There are many here who feel the want of religious reading and privileges; and if the ladies can furnish tracts, they will find cheerful distributors among the soldiers. Good officers and good soldiers make good regiments, and no small responsibility rests upon the people of Madison when it lays within their power to

---

[38] *Corres. Wis. Volunteers*, ii, p. 217.

WISCONSIN WOMEN IN THE WAR

give tone and character to those who under such particular circumstances are thrown in their midst.[39]

The Christian Commission undertook to answer this plea, and from all accounts was most successful in the distribution of tracts. One soldier writes that the children of the Sunday schools have supplied "nearly five hundred regiments, each with one thousand temperance and other tracts, in all amounting to nearly five hundred thousand. I entreat all under whose eyes this may chance to fall, to do all in their power by means of money and influence to forward the right kind of reading matter to the armies."[40]

Criticisms

The Christian Commission was not entirely exempt from criticism. Both the nature of the tracts and their method of distribution were adversely commented on. Nevertheless historical judgment admits that the motive was excellent, the movement timely, and the results of value to the armies; and in all its activities women had a considerable share.

---

[39] *Id.*, i, p. 208.
[40] *Id.*, x, p. 208.

Chapter XI

The Northwestern Sanitary Fair

In the autumn of 1863 a Sanitary Fair was held at Chicago, for which contributions were made by the entire Northwest. The proposal for this enterprise came from Mrs. Hoge and Mrs. Livermore, who had done so much to further the work of the Sanitary Commission. Mrs. Livermore thus describes the need that led to the inception of the fair:

> The continued need of money to obtain comforts and necessaries for the sick and wounded of our army has suggested to the loyal women of the North many and various devices for the raising of funds. Every city, town, and village has had its fair, festival, party, picnic, excursion, concert, etc., which have netted more or less to the cause of hospital relief, according to the population of the place, and the amount of energy and patriotism employed on the occasion. The need of money for this sacred purpose has suggested to many of the active and patriotic women of the Northwest the necessity of holding a grand Northwestern Fair in the fall, for the benefit of the Sanitary Commission. [41]

Preparations

The consent of the men in charge of the Commission having been obtained, these two indefatigable workers, Mrs. Hoge and Mrs. Livermore, issued a circular calling for a

---
[41] Livermore, pp. 410, 411.

WISCONSIN WOMEN IN THE WAR

woman's convention to be held in Chicago. Of these circulars, 10,000 were distributed throughout the Northwest, and as a result a convention of women delegates met in Chicago, September 1 and 2, and formally agreed to have a fair. Soon another circular was issued in an edition of 20,000, enumerating and classifying the articles desired. The aid of the press was requested and granted; an extensive correspondence with prominent public men was carried on, and thousands of letters were addressed to the women of the Northwest. Mrs. Livermore relates:

> In every principal town of the Northwest fair meetings were held, which resulted in handsome pledges, that were more than fulfilled. Towns and cities were canvassed for donations to the bazar and dining saloon. The whole Northwest was ransacked for articles, curios, unique, bizarre, or noteworthy, to add to the attractions of the "Curiosity Shop." Homes beautified with works of art, paintings, or statuary, were temporarily plundered of them for the art gallery, and all who possessed artistic, dramatic, decorative, or musical talent were pressed into the service of the evening entertainment. Executive women were chosen in every state, who freighted the mails with rousing appeals, or with suggestions born of their experience, frequently visiting different sections to conduct meetings in the interest of the great and noble enterprise. [42]

It would be outside the limits of this monograph to dwell upon the Fair in general; our interest concerns only the part which Wisconsin women played in this enterprise. Mrs. Henrietta Colt showed from the first a deep interest in the project, wherefore she was appointed a member of the executive committee,[43] together with Mrs. Harvey, Mrs. Salomon, Mrs. Carr, and other Wisconsin women.

---

[42] *Ibid*, p. 415.
[43] *History of Northwestern Soldiers' Fair* (Chicago, 1864), p. 8.

NORTHWESTERN SANITARY FAIR

German Women's Participation

The work of Mrs. Salomon in connection with the German department was conspicuous; the call for contributions reads:

> Mrs. Governor Salomon of Wisconsin, has kindly and generously consented to solicit and receive the contributions of the Germans for the Fair. These offerings will be sent together, will be arranged, displayed, and sold in a separate department, space being reserved for them exclusively, over which Mrs. Salomon consents to preside in person, throughout the Fair, assisted by ladies of her own selection. A most cordial and earnest invitation is extended to the German ladies of the Northwest to cooperate with Mrs. Salomon in her undertaking, with the assurance that every facility will be granted them for the display and sale of the beautiful handiwork and fancy wares in which they so greatly excel. [44]

This proposal was made only two or three weeks before the Fair, but the German women responded generally and generously, and the display of fancy-work, embroideries, etc., was astonishingly beautiful. Mrs. Salomon and her friends were so energetic in stirring up an interest in this department, that large contributions poured in from Milwaukee, Madison, Watertown, Manitowoc, and Sauk City. Among the articles contributed was a white silk embroidered flag, "surpassing anything in the way of embroidery, on exhibition;" it looked at the first glance more like painting than needle-work. It was the work of a Fond du Lac woman who wrought industriously with her needle for eighteen months to complete it. A portrait of Mozart adorned the centre of the flag, surrounded by musical in-

---
[44] *Ibid*, p. 12.

WISCONSIN WOMEN IN THE WAR

struments, while underneath were the notes of his celebrated opera, Don Giovanni. The flag was intended to grace the halls of a musical society; a subscription was instantly set on foot by the lovers of music to purchase it for the Chicago Philharmonic Society. The sum for its purchase, $150, was easily raised, and this unequalled piece of needle-work is now in the possession of that organization.

The whole amount of money raised in the German department was $6,000, of which amount the Germans of Wisconsin contributed $3,799. The patriotism of the German women during our great struggle was manifested on this occasion. As was well said by a contemporary writer, "As German sons, husbands, and brothers have mingled their life-blood with that of Americans, on almost every field of battle, it was well that their [the women's] offerings for the relief of sick and wounded soldiers, should be poured into the same receptacle, and the proceeds of their sale flow into the same treasury." [45]

Wisconsin Contributions

To Mrs. E. S. Carr was due the suggestion which resulted in the department known as the "Curiosity Shop." She proposed as one feature of this Fair to collect all the flags possible to procure, Federal and Confederate, which were used or taken by our soldiers in battle, together with other articles of an historic character or unusual value. This proved the most attractive of all the exhibits; among the battle-torn flags were six belonging to Wisconsin regiments. Wisconsin also sent a shackle taken from the ankle

---

[45] F. B. Goodrich, *The Tribute Book* (New York, 1865), p. 170.

NORTHWESTERN SANITARY FAIR

of a slave at Baton Rouge by Company F, Fourth Wisconsin; a representation of Hiawatha's wigwam, prepared at Green Bay; a beautiful collection of lichens from Albion; and a cross made from a piece of the Connecticut Charter Oak. Other curiosities from Wisconsin were a fine collection of minerals from Shullsburg; and another of iron, silver, and copper from Marquette; and an unusually good herbarium.

The art gallery also proved to be a very popular feature of the Fair; to this Wisconsin contributed her share of pictures. But more important than her contribution of these, was the presence of Mrs. Henrietta Colt, who presided over these treasures, assisted by several of the most attractive and cultivated women of the Northwest. To the uninitiated, and those not familiar with pictures, they gave information in so pleasant and agreeable a manner, that their services were in continual demand throughout the Fair. To all, their attentions were courteous and grateful, and it is doubtful if anyone remembers the exposition, without linking to it the bright and agreeable ladies who did so much to render a visit to the art gallery pleasant. [46]

The contributions of Wisconsin to this Fair were almost as heavy as those of Illinois; this was largely due to Mrs. Colt and the Milwaukee Aid Society. "Never can the nobleness of these ladies be forgotten. Living in a city which is an acknowledged mercantile rival to Chicago, they rose above all considerations of jealousy, and toiled to swell the pecuniary results of the Fair, which were to be devoted to the alleviations of the sufferers in the military hospitals. * * * And here let it be said that the

---

[46] *History N. W. Soldiers' Fair*, pp. 25, 35.

Milwaukee boxes were among the most elegant received. Lastly, costliness, beauty, and exquisite workmanship characterize them all."[47] With the boxes was likewise sent a draft for $1,000, collected through the efforts of the Milwaukee Aid Society.

From the women of Madison a generous contribution of various sorts was received. Among the articles donated was a sugar mill, bearing the wish that it might aid in grinding out the rebellion. With these gifts a sum of between four and five hundred dollars was sent, which had been collected by the women of the Madison Aid Society.

The success of the Northwestern Sanitary Fair was, to a considerable degree, due to the efforts of Wisconsin women.

---

[47] *Ibid*, pp. 57, 58.

Chapter XII

The Milwaukee Soldiers' Home and the Soldiers' Home Fair

In the spring of 1864, Mrs. Livermore, together with a number of other prominent Chicago women, decided that a soldiers' home was needed in Chicago. To raise the funds necessary for such a project, they arranged to hold another great fair. To further this plan they sent out as they had done in 1863 circulars soliciting supplies. Many prominent Milwaukee women favored this enterprise, but a few opposed it. Among those in the minority were three remarkable women—Mrs. Lydia Hewitt (now Mrs. Ely), Mrs. Hannah Vedder, and Mrs. E. L. Buttrick. These women had not been satisfied with the results of the Fair of 1863, and they feared that the new venture would be a failure. Moreover, they wanted a soldiers' home in Wisconsin. March 5, 1864, an old friend of the three ladies chanced to be on the same train, when they were returning from Chicago to Milwaukee after an unsatisfactory interview with Mrs. Livermore. His account of their conversation gives a sidelight on the origin of the Wisconsin Soldiers' Home Association:

They were having an animated discussion over their mission, which had continued for some time, and then the conversation ceased. Mrs. Hewitt looked out of the window for some minutes in silence. Then turning suddenly, as if she had caught an in-

WISCONSIN WOMEN IN THE WAR

spiration from the landscape, she exclaimed with vehemence, "I will not have anything to do with the Chicago proposition. It will be a failure. I am going to call a meeting to discuss the matter and will listen to what everyone has to say, but I will not allow anyone to deter me from my purpose or turn me from its object. I will have a soldiers' home in Milwaukee and will not stop until it is an accomplished fact. That's settled." "I will go with you," said Mrs. Buttrick. "So will I," said Mrs. Vedder. So on the following Monday a call was issued for a meeting of Milwaukee women, which resulted in the formation of the Wisconsin Soldiers' Home Association.[48]

Milwaukee Soldiers' Home

It is hardly just to attribute the Soldiers' Home at Milwaukee to the work of three women; it was rather the result of forces of which Mrs. Hewitt, Mrs. Buttrick, and Mrs. Vedder were the exponents. Perhaps the strongest force was the desire of the public that everything possible should be done for the soldiers at home, as well as in the field. Soldiers' homes, soldiers' orphans' asylums, pensions, and fairs were matters so much discussed, that the Wisconsin Soldiers' Home Association was only a part of a national movement. Its inception in Milwaukee was occasioned by the number of soldiers passing through on their way to and from the field. The following relates the objects of the society:

Impressed with the importance of adding to the comfort of the eighty thousand soldiers who were leaving or returning to our State, one year ago [April, 1864] the earnest women who composed this board, proposed with determination and misgivings and projected with hope, the Soldiers' Home. There was no lack of willingness on the part of the people to give,

---

[48] Ms. sent by Peter Van Vechten (Milwaukee, April, 1910).

MILWAUKEE SOLDIERS' HOME

simply the absence of a responsible and systematic channel, through which to dispense their cheerful bounties. A direct avenue was thus opened between the soldier in the State and the civilian, through which was free to pass all expression of good will in the shape of letters of sympathy, contributions of money, provisions, clothing, and medical stores.[49]

The women who thus organized the Wisconsin Soldiers' Home Association began their work with enthusiasm. Large rooms on West Water Street were rented, and arrangements made for receiving sick and wounded soldiers. It is significant that this was a women's movement, and that the men concerned in the management of the home acted merely as an advisory board.

From its start the home received the support and cordial good will of the people of Milwaukee and of the State at large, and soon the State itself granted to the home a charter, together with an appropriation of $5,000. The press, and railroad and telegraph companies cooperated with the Association, for they realized that "this home is not a wayside charity, or transient recreation, but a serious and permanent assumption of a sacred duty which we owe the defenders of our common country. It is food for the hungry, comfort for the cheerless, sympathy for the afflicted. It is a constant acknowledgment, that we too have duties, * * * which can neither be postponed nor evaded. It is an embodied declaration, that we at home acknowledge our obligations and are willing to share with

---

[49] "First Annual Report," in *Home Fair Journal*, a paper published in the interests of the Milwaukee Home Fair, May 20–July 8, 1865.

them [the soldiers] the arduous responsibilites of the hour."[50]

The home was managed upon a business basis, for the Association had regular meetings every two weeks, at which twenty-five women directors were present, and all details were carefully supervised. The officers were: president, Mrs. Lydia Hewitt; vice-presidents, Mrs. E. L. Buttrick, Mrs. J. H. Rogers, Mrs. J. J. Tallmadge, Mrs. S. S. Merrill; secretary, Mrs. A. J. Aikens; assistant secretary, Mrs. J. M. Kimball; treasurer, Mrs. D. A. Olin.[51] The home was in charge of a male superintendent and a matron; the president or one of the vice-presidents and a director were daily in attendance. "At the opening of the enterprise one building of limited capacity was occupied, such as our means would warrant, for from the first our motto has been 'owe no one' and the financiering has been at times fearfully close. As our contributions and necessities increased, we added another building, thus lessening the labor and increasing the alacrity with which meals could be provided and lodgings furnished."[52]

First Year's Results

The efficiency of this institution is shown in the results of its work during the first year. Within that time almost 3,000 soldiers were cared for, and 2,000 men, passing through the city, were fed at camps and depots, making a total of nearly 5,000 soldiers who were helped by the Association; 400 sick soldiers received surgical or medical

---

[50] *Ibid*, May 20, 1865.
[51] *Centennial Records*, pp. 74, 75.
[52] *Home Fair Journal*, May 20, 1865.

MILWAUKEE SOLDIERS' HOME

treatment, exclusive of those receiving special diet and nursing.

The brief and refreshing rest afforded by this institution to the sick, wounded, and worn soldier, was no doubt the direct means of saving many precious lives to the cause of the nation and to distant and anxious friends. Even the funeral expenses of the soldiers, who died at the home, were paid and the remains were as a rule forwarded to their homes. "When friendless, the ladies have stood by them until the last whisper ceased, as by those to whom they owe a debt of gratitude which no human tongue could tell. They went home to honored graves in our beautiful Forest Home. followed to the last by some of the ladies."

In March, 1865, the Senate and Assembly committees on Benevolent Institutions visited the Milwaukee Home and reported most favorably concerning its management. The closing paragraph of their report reads: "The committee extend to the ladies who compose this society, their most cordial approbation and commendation for their self-sacrificing devotion, their kindness and benevolence, their perseverence and industry, and also for the financial ability and business capacity which characterize their efforts in this behalf."[53]

Soldiers' Home Fair

It must not be forgotten, that from the beginning the Wisconsin Soldiers' Home Association looked toward the establishment of a permanent asylum for disabled soldiers. To achieve this result much money was needed, and Mrs.

---

[53] *Ibid.*

WISCONSIN WOMEN IN THE WAR

Hewitt and the directors thought that a great soldiers' home fair would best serve the purpose. So in the spring of 1864, the women of the Association made a canvass of Milwaukee and secured donations of many thousand feet of lumber and many days' labor for a Fair building.

Having the material for the building, Mrs. Hewitt went to an architect and asked him to draw a plan, and superintend the construction of the building. "Now, Mrs. Hewitt, you want three thousand dollars in money," he told her, whereupon the women of the Association decided to collect the sum needed. It was thought best to begin with a large subscription, so Mrs. Hewitt made up her mind to ask Alexander Mitchell for five hundred dollars; after having explained to him the need for it, he answered, "Tut, tut. What's that? Can't do it!" This reply was not encouraging, the case seemed hopeless, but Mrs. Hewitt tried again and very diplomatically said, "Mr. Mitchell, we expect to raise fifty thousand or sixty thousand dollars, and as we cannot spend all the money at once, it will be deposited in your bank." "Well, well, there's something in that—there's something in that. Put me down for five hundred. Nay, give me your paper." The paper was handed to him, and he became the first subscriber to the enterprise which resulted in the establishment of the Soldiers' Home. The only other $500 subscription was that of Mr. James Bonnell, a wholesale dry goods merchant.[54] Hundreds, however, contributed smaller amounts, until the sum for the building was secured.

---

[54] "Origin of the Milwaukee Soldiers' Home," in *Milwaukee News Annual* (Milwaukee, 1892–93), p. 51.

MILWAUKEE SOLDIERS' HOME

The Governor Aids

April 19, 1865, Governor Lewis issued the following proclamation:

The people of Wisconsin are second to none in patriotism or benevolence. No appeal for aid in any good cause has ever been made to them in vain. Knowing this fact, I feel that it is only necessary to call their attention to a good work to insure a proper response. The many sick and wounded soldiers returning from the field of battle * * * call loudly for our sympathy and help. They need and deserve a comfortable home and place of rest. With a view of providing such a home, the Legislature of this State at its last session, incorporated a benevolent institution to be known as the "Soldiers' Home," located at Milwaukee, and appropriated the sum of five thousand dollars to aid in its support. Further means are necessary to carry on the work. To supply them it is proposed to hold a State Fair at Milwaukee, commencing on the twenty-eighth day of June next, at which all who desire, may have an opportunity of contributing something to aid the wounded soldier. I would recommend this enterprise to the people as worthy of their aid and support and trust they will by their attendance and by contributing liberally of their means, which have been protected by the soldiers, make the Fair a success, and thus add to the soldiers' comfort. [55]

Wisconsin Towns Assist

Undoubtedly this proclamation had an effect upon the people of the State, but they were also stimulated into activity by the women of the Soldiers' Home Association, who visited nearly every portion of Wisconsin for this purpose. As a result many Soldiers' Home Fair societies were formed in the small towns for the sole purpose of getting

---
[55] *Home Fair Journal*, May 20, 1865.

WISCONSIN WOMEN IN THE WAR

money and contributions for the Fair. Affairs were also progressing well in Milwaukee; the canvassing committee soon secured ten thousand dollars, and the promise of large contributions for the entertainments and tables at the Fair.

It is impossible to give a complete list of the subscriptions and gifts received from the various parts of the State, for they came in great abundance from soldiers' aid societies, soldiers' home societies, sewing societies, churches, Sunday schools, private schools, orphans' homes, and such organizations as the "Hollanders," the "Good Templars," the "Spiritualists," and the German "Turners." Among communities contributing to the Fair, were the following cities and villages: Appleton, Beaver Dam, Beloit, Berlin, Delavan, Eau Claire, Fond du Lac, Grand Rapids, Green Bay, Green Lake, Hartford, Horicon, Iron Ridge, Janesville, Kilbourn City, La Crosse, Lake Mills, Lamertine, Lancaster, Manitowoc, Mauston, Mazomanie, Monroe, Oconomowoc, Omro, Oshkosh, Platteville, Plover, Prairie du Chien, Prairie du Sac, Prescott, Reedsburg, River Falls, Ripon, Rochester, Rubicon, Sheboygan, Somers, Sparta, Stevens Point, Troy, Two Rivers, Viroqua, Waterford, Watertown, Waukesha, Wausau, West Bend, Whitewater, Winneconne, and Woodland. [56]

The effort to make money for the Fair resulted in a perfect epidemic of entertainments such as festivals, picnics, dances, tableaux, concerts, and dramatic entertainments. The Germans of Milwaukee and other towns were especially active and gave a "Punch and Judy" show, a concert at Quentin's Park, and several other entertainments. The people living in the First Ward of Milwaukee gave a

---

[56] *Ibid*, June 3, 17, 28.

MILWAUKEE SOLDIERS' HOME

May-queen party which netted $144.08. At Beloit a soldiers' home festival was given by the pupils and teachers of "Union School, Number Two," at which novel and interesting tableaux, suggested by the war, were shown. At Sparta an old folks' concert was given. The Milwaukee Female College gave an operetta called the "Twin Sisters." The Madison Female Seminary engaged the City Hall for an exhibition "to be given by the teachers and students of the Seminary for the benefit of the Fair." A Prairie du Sac aid society gave an ice-cream festival, which included such amusements as fish-pond, ring-cake, and guess-cake. At Fond du Lac the little girls gave an ice-cream social; and at Ripon the small boys gave a dime show, to make money for the Fair. [57]

Among the donations received were some handsome conework from Manitowoc County: a piece of the towel used to bind Lincoln's head, from Miss Griswold of Madison; a statue called Violet; eight medallions of Lincoln from the women of Manitowoc, Plover, and Stevens Point, accompanied by yards of evergreen which was used in decorating the Fair building. The women of Osceola Mills sent a box of articles made of camelians, agates, and pine cones.

The Fair Building

In the meantime the building had been erected—a temporary structure, located south of the Chamber of Commerce, with a frontage of 300 feet on Main Street, and a depth of 135 feet, supporting an arched roof, fifty feet high, beneath which in the centre, was a floral temple. Running entirely around the main hall at a height of

---
[57] *Ibid*, May 20–July 8 inclusive.

WISCONSIN WOMEN IN THE WAR

twelve feet was a gallery, sixteen feet in width, reached by broad stairways at the rear end of the hall. The interior of the building was decorated with evergreens, flowers, and bunting, thus concealing the undressed pine lumber, of which it was constructed. The dining room was capable of seating 1,500 people; and hundreds of gas jets illuminated the building at night. [58]

The Exhibits

The scope of this Fair was very wide, for contributions had been solicited from every state in the Union, and even from prominent Americans living abroad. No profession or business was exempt; farmers, millers, merchants, photographers, and fruit-growers were among the contributors. Every department of commerce, industry, and agriculture was represented; and for the first time in Wisconsin's history an exhibit of paintings and statuary was shown. The Wisconsin scientific department contained a large number of botanical, geological, and zoological specimens, all of which were voted, during the first days of the Fair, to an educational institution in the State. The musical department and the department of arms and trophies were conspicuous for their completeness, and the public school and German departments were most interesting. [59]

Schools Contribute

The Department of Public Instruction issued the following proclamation to the teachers of the State:

On the twenty-eighth of June, 1865, and continuing two

---

[58] *Centennial Records*, p. 76.
[59] *Ibid*, p. 77.

MILWAUKEE SOLDIERS' HOME

weeks, will commence a grand State Fair for the purpose of raising funds to build a permanent Home for Wisconsin disabled soldiers. The contributions of three hundred thousand children and six thousand teachers in Wisconsin to this noble object, should amount to more than thirty thousand dollars. This cannot be done without prompt, energetic, enthusiastic, united, and systematic effort. Every true teacher's heart will feel the strong claims of the object upon all classes in the community. Never in the history of our State has there been presented a better opportunity for calling into exercise the noble sentiments and sympathy of the children, than the pressing and sacred obligations, which we all owe, in an especial manner, to our maimed, sick, shattered, and disabled soldiers, who are now coming back to receive our gratitude, and share the blessings for which we are indebted to their achievements and sacrifices.

You are the officers of the line, who are to command and direct the action of the grand army of three hundred thousand children in contributing to the School Department of the great Fair. Upon you more than upon any others, rests the responsibility and the labor of stimulating the children and gathering their offerings. The three hundred thousand children will rally about you with warm, generous, and tender hearts to receive the noble impulse. Their hands are eager for the grateful task, and you must lead them. If you delay or shrink or are indifferent all will fail, and the painful wound of ingratitude from friends at home, will pierce the hearts of our disabled soldiers, who have faced every danger unflinchingly in our cause. [60]

The method of collecting money for this department was a unique one. There was prepared a Soldiers' Home bank, to which every school child was supposed to contribute. The shares were ten cents each, and every child who contributed fifty cents or even less, was to have a cer-

---
[60] *Home Fair Journal*, May 20, 1865.

WISCONSIN WOMEN IN THE WAR

tificate of stock or a brick in the Soldiers' Home. The schools reported to the county or city superintendents, who made a report of the number of pupils and teachers in each township and the amount contributed. These reports were on exhibition at the Fair.

An appeal was also addressed to the children, which reads:

You ask, how can you get the money? We answer, work for it! earn it with your own hands. Do something for father and mother or older brothers and sisters; or work for some other persons; work for anybody on the farm, in the shop, at home, at school, in the store, knit, sew, hoe, plough, dig in the garden, drive cows or sheep, tend the baby, get better lessons, make better improvement in writing, be better boys and girls, do anything and everything good, honest, and right to get articles and money to give to the Soldiers' Home Fair. [61]

Both teachers and children took up the work with enthusiasm. Favorable reports were handed in, that the schools were becoming hives of warm-hearted industry. It must not be forgotten that women played a large part in the success of this department, for the teachers, who encouraged the children, were most of them women; the influence of the mothers at home had also much to do with the contributions of the children.

Special Features

Before the fair opened Mrs. Hewitt moved, that the kitchen and dining-room committees "be requested to proceed to business just the same as if the Fair had begun, and make provision for feeding 1,000 men per day. [62] The

---

[61] *Ibid.*
[62] *Ibid*, June 12.

MILWAUKEE SOLDIERS' HOME

motion was adopted, and the work of feeding the soldiers was placed in charge of the executive committee of the Soldiers' Home Association. During the progress of the Fair the Fifth Battery, and what remained of the Twenty-first, Twenty-fourth, Twenty-fifth, and Twenty-second regiments returned to Milwaukee. All of them were entertained at the Fair, and a number of the soldiers were lodged in the Fair building during their stay. [63]

A unique feature of the Fair was the Holland Kitchen, over which Mrs. Salomon presided. Here hundreds of people were fed each day; one contributor alone (Mrs. Van Vechten) made daily a barrel of doughnuts. [64] Another favorite department was the art gallery, which contained some very interesting features. Harriet Hosmer's statue of "Zenobia" attracted much attention, as did several of the Rogers groups, one of which, the "Bushwhacker," sold for forty dollars.

Perhaps the most interesting feature of the fair was Old Abe, the war eagle, which accompanied the Eighth Regiment throughout three years of service. He drew about him such crowds every day, that he became very tired, and had to be taken away for a rest. Not only the eagle but his photographs were on exhibition and thousands of them were sold.

Evening entertainments of various sorts attracted crowds of sight-seers. One of these, given by the women of Madison, was a series of grand tableaux. Entertainments known as Belshazzar's Feast, Statuary, The Baptism of

---

[63] *Illus. News Annual*, p. 51.
[64] Ms. letter from Mr. Van Vechten (April 25, 1910).

WISCONSIN WOMEN IN THE WAR

Pocohontas, and Mrs. Jarley's Wax Works occupied other evenings.

Financial Success

The Fair proved a greater success than was anticipated. At its close the Association found itself in possession of $139,604.80. It took several months to close up matters, pay expenses, sell the lumber of the building, and ascertain the net results; during all this time the president, Mrs. Hewitt, attended to every detail in person. It was finally found that $110,000 was on hand to build a permanent Soldiers' Home. Meanwhile, knowing that success was assured, the Association had purchased a lot for about $10,000, on which the future Wisconsin home for disabled soldiers was to be built.

Merged in Government Home

In July, 1866, the United States Government passed an act providing for national soldiers' homes. This stimulated several wise Milwaukeeans to make the attempt to secure one of these homes for their city. Dr. E. B. Wolcott was active in the matter, and with George Walker constituted a committee to visit Washington, and see what the Secretary of War proposed. Learning of the projected Wisconsin home, the authorities said if the funds and property of that institution were turned over to the Government to procure an appropriate site, one of the national homes would be located at Milwaukee.[65] The committee did not feel authorized to consent to these terms, since the

---

[65] *Ibid.*

THE UNITED STATES NATIONAL SOLDIERS' HOME, AT MILWAUKEE
From an early lithograph in possession of the Wisconsin Historical Society

MILWAUKEE SOLDIERS' HOME

money belonged to the women, but hastened home to present the proposition to the Soldiers' Home Association.

When Dr. Wolcott first presented the proposal of the Secretary of War to a meeting of the directors, there was with a single exception a unanimous opposition to its acceptance. The directors said that the fund had been raised for a Soldiers' Home, where their own care could be given to the sick and suffering soldier boys, such care as no paid Government employees would give, and that all would be subjected to the harsh regulations of Government service. The money had been raised by great effort and sacrifice, and it would be a betrayal of a trust to turn it over to the Government. One quiet woman, who had listened to all their arguments, but who had the independent judgment to see things in their larger aspect, suggested that this was a matter not to be decided by sentiment. She set forth that most of their money would be needed for the proposed building, that it would mean a constant struggle for years to provide for its maintenance, and a tax upon the energies of more than one generation of Milwaukee women. Moreover, the National Home would be of great value to their city, and in the end Wisconsin soldiers would be better cared for under Government than private auspices.

These arguments appealed to the broad-minded directors of the Association; and at the next meeting, which was largely attended by the Association membership, it was voted to accept the Government's proposal, and merge their home in a national one.[66]

---

[66] Personal recollections by A. W. Kellogg of Milwaukee, concerning the attitude and remarks of his wife at the directors' meeting.

WISCONSIN WOMEN IN THE WAR

With the transfer in July, 1867, of the property to the board of commissioners of the National Asylum for Disabled Soldiers, the Wisconsin Solders' Home Association ceased to exist. Dr. Wolcott and Mrs. Hewitt were a local committee to choose the site, and selected the beautiful grounds that are now the pride of the city.

During the period of its activity (from April 1864 to July 1866) the Wisconsin Soldier's Home sheltered 31,650 soldiers, of whom more than 1,000 received medical treatment and of that number only twenty-eight died. [67]

The Wisconsin Soldiers' Home and the Milwaukee Home Fair were promoted and managed by women, and the remarkable energy and business ability of Mrs. Lydia Hewitt and her assistants carried both these projects to success. The whole episode was part of the uprising of the women of the North, and shows the native ability and tireless persistency of the American woman of 1865.

---

[67] *Illustrated News Annual*, p. 53.

INDEX

AID SOCIETIES, described, 22-46; statistics of, 46-48; reawakened, 54.
Aikens, Mrs. J. J., director of Soldiers' Home, 164.
Albion, aids Chicago fair, 159.
Alert Club, gathers funds, 25.
Alexandria (Va.), soldiers at, 77; hospitals, 113-115.
Allotment commissioners, duties, 121, 122.
Almond, supplies from, 54.
American Magazine, cited, 18, 110.
Appleton, supplies from, 46, 54; aids Home fair, 168.
Arkansas Post (Ark.), captured, 53.
Arlington Heights (Va.), Wisconsin troops at, 105.
ARMIES: Cumberland, threatened with scurvy, 45; hospitals for, 39, 52.
Atlanta (Ga.), Wisconsin soldiers at, 77.
Aubery, J. M., *Thirty-sixth Wisconsin Infantry*, 27.

BACON, Georgeanna W., and Howland, Eliza W., *Letters of a Family*, 111.
Baker, Mrs. —, aid acknowledged, 72.
Baraboo, supplies from, 54.
Baton Rouge (La.), Wisconsin soldiers at, 159.
BATTLES: Bull Run, 31; Chancellorsville, 41, 62; Fort Donelson, 112; Fredericksburg, 41, 62; Pittsburg Landing, 34, 36, 112; Resaca, 55; near Richmond, 37; Shiloh, 147.
Bear Creek (Miss.), Wisconsin troops at, 104.
Beaver Dam, aids Home fair, 168; rifle company, 12.
Beloit, flag made at, 9; supplies from, 32, 43, 46, 54; soldiers' families at, 63, 95; aids Home fair, 168, 169.
Bennett, Mrs. James, aid acknowledged, 83.

INDEX

Benton Barracks (Mo.), hospital at, 123.
Berlin, supplies from, 31, 54; aids Home fair, 168.
Bickerdyke, Mrs. Mary A., in Milwaukee, 55-57.
Billings, J. H., *Hard Tack and Coffee*, 7, 30, 31.
Bissell, Katherine, in Christian Commission work, 152.
Bloor, Alfred, letters from, 54, 59, 60.
Bonnell, James, contributes to Home fair, 166.
Bristol, supplies from, 44.
Brockett, L. P., and Vaughan, M. C., *Women's Work in the Civil War*, 49-53, 56, 125, 126, 130-132, 134.
Brodhead, Alert Club at, 24, 25.
Browning, Elizabeth Barrett, "Parting Lovers," 17.
Burnell, K. A., in Christian Commission work, 151.
Burton, R. W., superintends Orphans' Home, 146.
Burton, Mrs. R. W., matron of Orphans' Home, 146.
Butler, Anna B. (ed.), *Centennial Records of Women of Wisconsin*, 144, 146, 164, 170.
Buttrick, Mrs. E. L., plans Soldiers' Home, 161, 162; vice-president of association, 164.

CAIRO (Ill.), hospital at, 52, 119; convalescents, 131; Christian Commission work, 152.
Cameron, Don. C. See Webster and Cameron.
Cameron, Simon, secretary of war, 19.
CAMPS: Scott, 10, 15. Randall, banquet at, 11-13; troops, 68, 115, 153; Confederate prisoners, 87; hospital, 144. Reno, 56. Utley, 7. Washburn, 56.
Cape Girardeau (Mo.), hospitals at, 123-126.
Carr, Mrs. E. S., aids Chicago fair, 156, 158.
Carter, Walter S., organizes Wisconsin Christian Commission, 150.
Chicago, needs soldiers' home, 161; newspapers, 52; fair at, 155-160; Christian Commission, 150; Philharmonic Society, 158; Sanitary Commission, 20, 41, 43 45, 47, 51, 54, 56, 57. See also Northwestern Sanitary Commission.
Chilton, soldiers' families at, 65.
Christian Commission. See United States Christian Commission.
Clinton Junction, Harveys at, 118.

INDEX

Clothing, furnished by government, 31, 32; contracts for, 54, 57–60.
Collins, Mason, enlists, 103.
Collins, Sarah, desires to enlist, 103.
Colt, Joseph S., Milwaukee lawyer, 50.
Colt, Mrs. Henrietta, in Aid Society work, 49, 54, 55, 57, 59, 60; in the South, 51–54; Washington, 57, 59; aids Chicago fair, 156; characterized, 50, 51.
Columbia County, women farmers in, 83.
Columbus (Miss.), wounded at, 52.
Columbus (Wis.), supplies from, 54.
Confederate prisoners, at Camp Randall, 87, 88.
Corinth (Miss.), hospital at, 131.
Correspondence of Wisconsin Volunteers, 5, 8, 10–17, 28, 29, 31, 32, 35, 37, 38, 40, 64–67, 88, 93, 94, 97, 99–102, 104–107, 109, 112, 115, 117, 119, 120, 122, 153, 155.
Cottage Grove, provides for banquet, 11.
Culbertson, Dr. Howard, in charge of Harvey Hospital, 143, 144.
Culver, L. D., aid acknowledged, 103.
Curtis, Gen. Samuel R., aids Mrs. Harvey, 125.

Dane County, banquets soldiers, 11–13; soldiers from, 76.
Daughters of the regiments, 100–102.
Delafield, Mrs. Louisa, in Milwaukee Aid Society, 49.
Delavan, supplies from, 54; aids Home fair, 168; woman from, 152.
Dickinson, Anna, services, 118.
Dix, Dorothea, pioneer nurse, 110, 118.
Doolittle, Judge James R., letter for, 121.
Doty, Mrs. —, aid acknowledged, 72, 79.
Dousman, Mrs. —, in Milwaukee Aid Society, 49.
Draper, J. W., *Civil War in America*, 149.
Dunn County, resident, 100.

East Delavan, supplies from, 46.
Eau Claire, aids Home fair, 168.
Eldred, Mrs. H. J., aid acknowledged, 74, 80, 87.

[179]

INDEX

Elkhorn, supplies from, 46.
Ellenboro, soldier from, 103.
Ellsworth, Col. E. E., killed, 149.
Ely, Mrs. —. See Mrs. Lydia Hewitt.
Enlistments, how stimulated, 2-6.
Ensign, Mrs. Annie Johnson, in Christian Commission work, 152.
Ewbank, Hannah, daughter of Seventh regiment, 102.

FARMS, operated by women, 78-83.
Fisk, Gen. Clinton B., headquarters, 52.
Fite, E. D., *Social and Industrial Conditions during the Civil War*, 78, 85, 86, 147-449; "Agricultural Development of the West," 78.
Fitzgerald, Mrs. —, aid acknowledged, 71.
Flags, presented to regiments, 7-10; at Chicago fair, 158.
Fond du Lac, aids fairs, 157, 168, 169.
FORTS: Donelson, 112; Pickering, 131; Sumter, 1, 9, 118.
Fox Lake, supplies from, 46, 54.
Freedmen, schools for, 151.

GAYLORD, Adj. Gen. Augustus, hears of governor's death, 120.
Geneva, soldiers' families at, 65.
Germans, aid fairs, 157, 158, 168.
Gilbert, Frank L., oration, 146, 147.
Ginseng, gathered for sale, 65.
Good Templars, aid Home fair, 168.
Goodrich, F. B., *The Tribute Book*, 158.
Grand Rapids, aids Home fair, 168.
Grant, Gen. Ulysses S., army threatened with scurvy, 43, 45, aids Mrs. Harvey, 131.
Grant County, flag from, 8; supplies, 29; Veterans' Association, 70, 74.
Green, Reuben, mentioned, 3.
Green Bay, quilt from, 26, 27; supplies, 46, 54; aids fairs, 159; 168.
Green County, provision for soldiers' families, 64.
Griswold, Miss —, donation, 169.

INDEX

HADLEY, Miss A. M., Wisconsin nurse, 112.
Hammond, Gen. William A., in charge of hospitals, 121.
Harrisburg (Pa.), Wisconsin Sixth Infantry at, 99.
Hartford, supplies from, 46; aids Home fair, 168.
Harvey, Mrs. Cordelia A. P., early life, 118; husband's death, 119-121; sanitary agent, 122, 123; in Southern hospitals, 123-133; visits to Lincoln, 132, 134-143; founds Orphans' Home, 144 147; aids Chicago fair, 156; portrait, frontispiece.
Harvey, Gov. Louis P., calls for supplies, 34; distributes aid, 36; marriage, 118; elected governor, 118, 119; death, 120, 147; hospital named for, 141.
Harvey Hospital, supplies for, 56, 57; founded, 141, 143, 144; site, 147.
Harvey Zouaves, equipped, 119.
"Havelocks," uselessness of, 21.
Hazel Green, supplies from, 46.
Helena (Ark.), hospitals at, 126.
Henshaw, Mrs. S. E., *Our Branch and its Tributaries*, 10, 21, 37, 39, 42-45, 48, 51.
Hewitt, Mrs. Lydia, plans Soldiers' Home, 161, 162; president of association, 164, 166, 172, 174, 176.
Hoge, Mrs. A. H., in Southern hospitals, 51, 52, 75, 76; sanitary work, 41, 56; promotes fair, 155.
Hollanders, aid Home fair, 168.
Holton, E. D., allotment commissioner, 121.
Home Fair Journal, 163 165, 167-169, 171, 172.
Hopkins, Mrs. B. F., edits pamphlet, 89.
Horicon, aids Home fair, 168.
Hosmer, Harriet, sculptor, 173.
Hospitals, bad conditions in, 108, 109, 112, 113, 116; Governor Harvey visits, 119, 120; Wisconsin women in, 51-53, 112-116, 123 133; in Northern states, 132, 134-144; matrons for, 115, 116.
"Housewives," furnished soldiers, 27.
Howe, Elias, inventor, 85.
Howe, Timothy O., letter from, 12; petitions for hospital, 134.
Howland, Eliza W. See Bacon and Howland.

[181]

INDEX

Hoyt, Mrs. J. W., edits pamphlet, 89.
Hudson, soldiers' families at, 65.
Hurlbutt, Trume, mentioned, 3.

ILLINOIS, contributions from, 46-48; suffers from drought, 43.
Ilsley, Miss Lottie, in Milwaukee Aid Society, 58.
Iowa, women farmers in, 80; supplies from, 43, 46, 47.
Iron Ridge, aids Home fair, 168.
Ironton (Ky.), hospital at, 126.
Island Number Ten, captured, 87.

JACKSON, Mrs. Margaret, in Aid Society work, 49.
Jackson, Mrs. William, in Milwaukee Aid Society, 58.
Jackson (Miss.), hospital at, 131.
Janesville, entertains regiment, 14; supplies from, 27, 28, 54; aids Home fair, 168; Light Guard, 12; *Gazette*, 107.
Jefferson, soldiers' families at, 65.
Jeffersonville, supplies from, 32.
Johnson, Rossiter, *History of War of Secession*, 18.

KELLEY, Mrs. C. V., in Milwaukee Aid Society, 58.
Kellogg, Mrs. A. W., influence on Soldiers' Home directors, 175.
Kenosha, banquets regiment, 14, 15; soldiers' families at, 75; early settlers, 118.
Kentucky, invaded, 36.
Keyes, Elisha W., aid acknowledged, 103.
Kilbourn City, soldiers' families at, 65; aids Home fair, 168.
Kimball, Mrs. J. M., director of Soldiers' Home, 164.
King, Gen. Rufus, at Milwaukee, 10.
Kingston, reception at, 13.
Knitting for soldiers, 29, 30.

LA CROSSE, regiments feasted at, 11; aids Home fair, 168.
Lafonte, Mrs. —, aids soldier's family, 70.
La Grange (Mo.), hospital at, 131.
Lake Mills, soldiers from, 103; aids Home fair, 168.
Lake Monona, hospital near, 143.
Lamertine, aids Home fair, 168.

INDEX

Lancaster, flag made at, 8; aids Home fair, 168.
Leindecker, Mrs. Isabel, anecdote of, 69 71.
Letters, for soldiers and their families, 92-98.
Lewis, Gov. James T., plans Orphans' Home, 145; aids Home fair, 167.
Lincoln, Abraham, call for troops, 18; authorizes Sanitary Commission, 19; medallions of, 169; interviewed by Mrs. Harvey, 135-142.
Lint, methods of preparing, 25, 26.
Little Rock (Ark.), Christian Commission at, 152.
Livermore, Mrs. Mary E., sanitary work, 41, 45, 52, 56; promotes fairs, 155, 161; visits Wisconsin, 80-82; *My Story of the War*, 19, 20, 52, 82, 93, 108, 155, 156.
Lodi, soldiers' families at, 67.
Louisville (Ky.), woman worker at, 49.
Love, William De Loss, *Wisconsin in the War of the Rebellion*, 7, 10, 54, 64, 123.
Lyon, Col. William P., incident concerning, 106, 107.
Lyon, Mrs. William P., with the army, 106, 107.

McClure, Mrs. —, in Milwaukee Aid Society, 49.
McIntyre, G. H., aid acknowledged, 130.
Madison, soldiers feasted at, 11-13; supplies from, 34, 43, 46; contributions, 63, 145, 153, 157, 160, 173; hospital at, 131, 143; aids soldiers' families, 68, 69; cares for prisoners, 88; clothing contract at, 58; Ladies Union League, 68, 89, 90; seminary, 169; newspaper, 75; interview at, 83. See also Camp Randall.
Manitowoc, mentioned, 71; aids fairs, 157, 168, 169.
Manitowoc County, donation from, 169.
Marquette, daughter of regiment from, 102; aids Chicago fair, 159.
Maryland, invaded, 36.
Mauston, aids Home fair, 168.
Mazomanie, supplies from, 54; aids Home fair, 168.
Melrose, aid society at, 42.
Memphis (Tenn.), hospitals at, 53, 126, 129-131; supplies for, 51; Christian Commission at, 151, 152.

INDEX

Menasha Wooden Ware Company, employs women, 85.
Menomonie, daughter of regiment from, 100.
Merrill, Mrs. S. S., director of Soldiers' Home, 164.
Michigan, drought in, 43; supplies from, 46.
Middleton, provides for banquet, 11.
Milwaukee, flag presented at, 10; regiments, 11, 15-17; supplies from, 29, 30, 34-36, 43, 44, 46, 47, 54; hospital at, 143, 144; aids Chicago fair, 157 160; Soldiers' Home, 161-176; government home, 174-176; Chamber of Commerce, 55; College, 169; cemetery, 165; park, 168; zouaves, 28; *News Annual*, 166; *Sunday Telegraph*, 26, 76; *Wisconsin*, 34. See also Wisconsin Aid Society.
Milwaukee & Prairie du Chien Railroad, gives transportation, 58.
Minnesota, soldier from, 128.
Missouri, invaded, 36, 123.
Mitchell, Alexander, contributes to fair, 166.
Monroe, aids Home fair, 168.
Moore, Frank, *Women of the War*, 57, 76, 148.
Mosby, John S., guerrilla leader, 59.
Mound City (Ark.), hospital at, 119.

NATIONAL ASYLUM for Disabled Soldiers, located at Milwaukee, 174-176.
National Tribune, cited, 25.
Nazro, Mrs. John, in Milwaukee Aid Society, 49.
New Orleans (La.), hospitals at, 132, 137.
New York city, Christian Commission organized at, 148.
Northwestern Sanitary Commission, fair, 155-160; *Reports*, 47, 51. See also Chicago.

OAK CREEK, supplies from, 54.
Oconomowoc, aids Home fair, 168.
Oconto, soldiers' families at, 65.
Ogden, Mrs. —, in Milwaukee Aid Society, 49.
Ohio, soldiers from, 39.
"Old Abe," at Home fair, 173.
Olin, Mrs. D. A., director of Soldiers' Home, 164.
Olmstead, Frederick Law, in Sanitary Commission, 40.

INDEX

Omro, aids Home fair, 168.
Osceola Mills, donations from, 169.
Oshkosh, regiments feasted at, 11; supplies from, 46; army nurse, 113; aids Home fair, 168.

PADUCAH (Ky.), hospital at, 119.
Pennsylvania, invaded, 36.
Perrine family, in Kenosha, 118.
Peterson, Belle, enlists in army, 103.
Philadelphia, women join Christian Commission, 150.
Pittsburg Landing (Tenn.), hospital at, 119, 120. See also Battles.
Platteville, contribution to soldiers' families, 63; aids Home fair, 168.
Plover, aids Home fair, 168, 169.
Pollis, Mrs. H. A., letter from, 42.
Port Fulton, supplies from, 32.
Port Washington, supplies from, 55.
Portage, supplies from, 54.
Porter, Mrs. Eliza, petitions for Northern hospitals, 134, 135.
Prairie du Chien, supplies from, 46; soldiers' families at, 82; hospital, 143, 144; aids Home fair, 168; Sacred Heart Academy, 144.
Prairie du Sac, supplies from, 54; aids Home fair, 168, 169.
Prescott, aids Home fair, 168.
Prices, in war times, 73, 74.

QUARTERLY *Journal of Economics*, cited, 78.
Quincy (Ill.), hospitals at, 139.
Quiner, E. B., collects clippings, 5; *Military History of Wisconsin*, 34, 122, 134.
Quinine, used in army, 27, 33.

RACINE, camp at, 7; flag described, 8; dinner at, 11; supplies from, 31, 43, 44; sanitary agent, 112; soldiers, 37.
Randall, Gov. Alexander W., message of, 1, 2.
Read, Thomas B., "Wagoner of the Alleghanies," cited, 61.
Ream's Station (Va.), prisoner taken at, 75.

INDEX

Rebellion Records, 110, 116.
Recruits, drilled, 6, 7.
Reedsburg, aids Home fair, 168.
Retrenchment, the Duty of Women of the North, 89 91.
Rhodes, James Ford, *History of the United States*, 62.
Richland County, provides for soldiers' families, 66, 85.
Riehr, Mrs. C. A., in Milwaukee Aid Society, 49.
Ripon, cavalry company, 31; soldiers' families at, 65; supplies from, 55; aids Home fair, 168, 169.
Rittenhouse, Edward, aid acknowledged, 144.
River Falls, aids Home fair, 168.
RIVERS: Mississippi, 125, 139, 151; Tennessee, 147.
Robinson, Mrs. Mary Burnell, in Christian Commission work, 151, 152.
Rochester, aids Home fair, 168.
Rock County, officials in, 118.
Rogers, Earl M., cited, 33.
Rogers, Mrs. J. H., director of Soldiers' Home, 164.
Rogers, John, sculptor, 173.
Rolla (Mo.), Wisconsin troops at, 105, 106; hospital, 126.
Rood, H. W., "One little Mother," 76-78; *Company E and the Twelfth Wisconsin*, 3-7.
Rubicon, aids Home fair, 168.

SAGE, gathered for sale, 85.
St. Louis (Mo.), Wisconsin troops at, 37, 104, 105; hospital, 129; medical director, 127-129; convalescents, 131; sanitary agent, 122, 123, 125; donations for, 49, 56, 57; Sanitary Commission, 54. See also Western Sanitary Commission.
Salem, supplies from, 46.
Salisbury (N. C.), prison at, 75.
Salomon, Gov. Edward, appoints sanitary agents, 122; letters for, 125, 129; desires hospitals, 134.
Salomon, Mrs. Edward, visits Southern hospitals, 105, 106; edits pamphlet, 89; aids fairs, 156, 157, 173.
Sanitary Commission. See United States Sanitary Commission.
Sanitary Reporter, cited, 45.
Sauk City, aids Chicago fair, 157.

INDEX

Sauk County rifles, leave home, 13.
Savannah (Tenn.), Governor Harvey drowned at, 120.
Schuyler, Louisa Lee, in Sanitary Commission, 22–24, 118.
Scurvy, attempts to prevent, 42–46.
Selkirk, Mrs. James, aid acknowledged, 124.
Sewing-machines, use of, 85, 86.
Sheboygan, supplies from, 43, 46, soldiers' families at, 65; aids Home fair, 168; *Telegram*, 9.
Sherman, Gen. William T., commands on Mississippi, 51, 52.
Shopiere, Harveys at, 118.
Showalter, Mrs. Martha, aid acknowledged, 8, 73, 102.
Shullsburg, aids Chicago fair, 159.
Simmons, Mary E., aid acknowledged, 9, 28, 29, 42, 95.
Singer sewing-machines, 86.
Skinner, Mary E., aid acknowledged, 147.
Soldiers' Orphans' Home (Madison), described, 144–147.
Solomon, Jim, mentioned, 3.
Somers, aids Home fair, 168.
Sparta, soldiers' families at, 65; aids Home fair, 168, 169.
Spiritualists, aid Home fair, 168.
Spring Prairie, supplies from, 44.
Stanton, Edwin M., secretary of war, 136, 137.
Stevens Point, aids Home fair, 168, 169.
Sun Prairie, provides for banquet, 11.
Swift Hospital, at Prairie du Chien, 144.

TALLMADGE, Mrs. J. J., director of Soldiers' Home, 164.
Tarbell, Ida M., "The American Woman," 18, 110.
Teale, Mrs. —, cited, 40.
Tennessee, battles in, 34, 36, 123.
Thwaites, R. G., "Cyrus Hall McCormick and the Reaper," 78; *Wisconsin*, 143.
Troy, aids Home fair, 168.
Trumbull, Henry C., *War Memoirs of a Chaplain*, 92, 94.
Turner, Mrs. —, army nurse, 112.
Turn-Verein, members aid Home fair, 168.
Tustin, soldiers' families at, 75.

INDEX

Tuttle, C. R., *History of Wisconsin*, 50, 53, 120, 126, 130-132.
Two Rivers, aids Home fair, 168.

UNITED STATES, postal facilities for army, 93, 94; Census *Reports*, 83, 84.
United States Christian Commission, purposes, 148, 149; supplies, 114, 153, 154; women's part in, 150-152; criticized, 155; Wisconsin branch, 150, 151; *Ladies' Auxiliaries*, 150.
United States Sanitary Commission, described, 18-20; forwards supplies, 33, 34, 39, 40, 45; opposed, 37, 38; fights scurvy, 42 46; revived, 41, 42; relief for soldiers' families, 59, 60; Wisconsin agent, 112; Milwaukee branch, 49-60; statistics, 46 48; holds fair, 155 160; *Bulletin*, 20, 22, 27, 46, 54, 60; *Documents*, 40. See also Aid Societies, Northwestern Sanitary Commission, and Western Sanitary Commission.

VAN VALKENBURG, Mrs. Susannah, services, 113 115.
Van Vechten, Peter, aid acknowledged, 162, 173.
Vaughan, M. C. See Brockett and Vaughan.
Vedder, Mrs. Hannah, plans Soldiers' Home, 161, 162.
Vernon County, enlistment in, 5.
Vicksburg, captured, 36; supplies for, 45, 51; Grant besieges, 131; hospitals at, 132, 139; Christian Commission work, 152.
Virginia, Wisconsin women in camps of, 107.
Viroqua, aids Home fair, 168; *Leader*, 33.

WALKER, GEORGE, secures government home, 174.
Walker, Mrs. George, presents flag, 10.
Wallin, A. C., aid acknowledged, 82.
Washington (D. C.), hospitals at, 31; Mrs. Harvey, 132, 134-142, 145; Milwaukee committee, 174.
Waterman, J. H., "Rosendale Squad," 25.
Waterford, aids Home fair, 168.
Watertown, supplies from, 28, 46; aids fairs, 157, 168.
Waukesha, soldiers' family at, 72; aids Home fair, 168.
Waupaca, patriotic teacher at, 86, 87; interviews by author, 71, 72, 79, 80, 87.
Wausau, aids Home fair, 168.

INDEX

Waushara County, enlistments in, 6; women farmers, 79, 80.
Wauwatosa, supplies from, 55.
Webster, Dan, and Cameron, Don C., *Story of First Wisconsin Battery*, 5–7.
West Bend, aids Home fair, 168.
West Milwaukee, collects vegetables, 44.
Western Sanitary Commission, supplies, 125, 131. See also St. Louis.
Weyauwega, soldiers' families at, 80.
Wheeler & Wilson sewing machines, 85.
Whitewater, supplies from, 43, 44; soldiers' families at, 65; aids Home fair, 168.
Williams, Serg.—, death of wife, 107.
Williamsburg (Va.), Wisconsin soldiers at, 77.
Wilson, Eliza, daughter of Fifth regiment, 100–102.
Wilson, Mrs. Teresa, "A Memory of War Times," 74.
Wilson, William, Wisconsin senator, 100.
Windsor, supplies from, 44.
Winneconne, aids Home fair, 168.
Wisconsin, sparse population, 42, 47; adjutant-general, 65; quartermaster-general, 58; secretary of state, 59; surgeon-general's *Report*, 144; hospitals in, 132, 143; supplies from, 43–48; provision for soldiers' families, 63–66; sanitary agents, 116, 117, 122–133; women's occupations in, 78–84; grant to Soldiers' Home, 163; aids Chicago fair, 158–160; schools aid Home fair, 170–172; soldiers, 147; 1st Infantry, 10, 14, 32; 2nd Cavalry, 132; 3d Cavalry, 104; 4th Infantry, 11–13, 65, 159; 5th Battery, 173; 5th Infantry, 11–13, 100–102; 6th Infantry, 32, 33, 99, 105; 7th Infantry, 14, 31, 32, 102, 104, 107; 8th Infantry, 33, 104, 106, 173; 11th Infantry, 104; 13th Infantry, 106; 19th Infantry, 87, 88; 21st Infantry, 173; 22nd Infantry, 175; 24th Infantry, 16, 17, 173; 25th Infantry, 173; 36th Infantry, 27.
Wisconsin Christian Commission, 150, 151.
Wisconsin Historical Society, library, 5; *Proceedings*, 78.
Wisconsin Soldiers' Aid Society, 49–60; *Report*, 57, 58, 60.
Wisconsin Soldiers' and Citizens' Biographical Record, 114.
Wisconsin State Journal, cited, 2.

INDEX

Wolcott, Dr. E. B., surgeon-general, 34, 143, 144; secures government home, 174-176.
Woman's Central Association of Relief, formed, 18, 22.
Woodland, aids Home fair, 168.
Wording, W. E., sanitary agent, 112.
Wording, Mrs. W. E., acts as nurse, 112.

YOUNG'S POINT (La.), hospital at, 52, 131, 132.